How To:
$10M

ISBN: 979-8321890103

Imprint: Independently published

Copyright 2024, William Brown

This book was produced with Write Business Results Limited.
For more information on their business book and marketing
services, please visit www.writebusinessresults.com
or contact the team via info@writebusinessresults.com.

 WRITE BUSINESS RESULTS

SELL YOUR KNOWLEDGE
AND MAKE MILLIONS

HOW TO: $10M

WILLIAM BROWN

Acknowledgements

To my parents, who raised me with the belief that I could do anything I put my mind to and worked hard for. There's no way I'd be where I am today without that belief you instilled in me. Thank you for always supporting me, no matter the venture I pursued.

To my clients both new and old, who put their trust in me to help them build and grow their businesses. Without you, I'd be without a mission and a calling in life. I'm constantly excited and thankful to help you reach the heights that you deserve to reach.

Contents

Foreword

It is with great pride and enthusiasm that I introduce you to the remarkable work of a remarkable entrepreneur.

In the world of business and entrepreneurship, there are few things more rewarding than seeing someone who takes the knowledge, insights and strategies they've learned and use them to forge a path to extraordinary success. This book is a testament to the power of mentorship, dedication and the relentless pursuit of one's dreams. As someone who has dedicated my life to helping business owners realise their entrepreneurial potential, I am continually inspired by the stories of those who take the knowledge and guidance they receive and turn it into something truly extraordinary.

As the author of *Breeding Gazelles* and *Turnover is Vanity, Profit is Sanity*, I have had the privilege of working with countless entrepreneurs, each with their own unique vision and journey. I've witnessed firsthand the incredible potential of those who dare to dream big and take bold action. Today, I am honoured to introduce you to William Brown, a student of mine who embodies the very essence of what it means to be an entrepreneur. In this book, William shares his journey and the strategies he's used to build an information product business and grow it to over ten million dollars in revenue.

But this book is not just about Will's journey; it's a blueprint for anyone who aspires to achieve similar success in the world of selling information. It's a roadmap filled with actionable insights, practical advice and invaluable lessons learned from the trenches of entrepreneurship.

Building a business that generates ten million dollars in revenue is no small feat. It requires a unique blend of creativity, determination and strategic thinking. It's about identifying a market need, crafting a compelling offer, and executing with precision. And it's about learning from failures, adapting to challenges and staying the course even when the path is uncertain. Will has navigated this journey with grace and resilience, and his story serves as a source of inspiration for all aspiring entrepreneurs. He has not only achieved financial success, but has also created a business that empowers others and adds value to countless lives.

In the following pages, you will discover the strategies and tactics that Will used to build his information product empire.

From identifying profitable niches to creating irresistible offers, from mastering marketing and sales, to scaling operations, Will leaves no stone unturned. This book is a treasure trove of knowledge that will empower you to embark on your own journey to ten million dollars, and beyond.

What sets this book apart is not just the wealth of information it contains, but the fact that it is written by someone who has been in the trenches, faced challenges head-on, and emerged victorious. Will understands the realities of entrepreneurship, and their insights are battle-tested and proven. As you read through these pages, I encourage you to take notes, highlight key takeaways and, most importantly, take action. The knowledge contained within these chapters has the power to transform your business and your life. But it is up to you to put it into practice.

I have no doubt that Will's journey and this book will inspire you to dream bigger, work smarter and achieve greater success than you ever thought possible. Whether you're just starting your entrepreneurial journey or looking to take your existing business to new heights, the wisdom within these pages will be your guiding light.

So, without further ado, I invite you to dive into the world of Will and discover the secrets to building an information product business and growing it into multiple millions of dollars. As you embark on this journey, remember that the path to success is not always easy, but with the right guidance and unwavering determination, you too can achieve greatness.

To Will, I offer my heartfelt congratulations and deepest respect for your achievements. Your story is a testament to the power of ambition, hard work and the relentless pursuit of excellence. I am honoured to have played a small part in your journey, and I am excited to see the impact your wisdom will have on aspiring entrepreneurs around the world.

To our readers, I say this: prepare to be inspired, educated and empowered. The journey to ten million dollars begins here.

Dan Bradbury

Author of *Breeding Gazelles* and *Turnover is Vanity, Profit is Sanity*

AudioBook

Did you know that...

**Listening and Reading Simultaneously Can Improve Focus
and Comprehension by <u>30% - 50%</u>**

Get your **FREE** *Audiobook now!*
SCAN THE QR CODE

Introduction

Are you ready to have the best job in the world? I mean it. In this book I'm going to share everything I've learned about building an incredibly successful business and living an amazing life.

How would you feel if you had full control over what you work on, where you work on it, when you work on it, and with whom you work on it? That's the dream, right? Total control to live your life the way *you* want.

In this book, you'll learn how to create a business that allows you to have full control over all of those elements of what we call "work", and by the time you've ticked those boxes you'll have the best job in the world – if we can call such a thing a "job" that is. It will feel more like a blessing because you'll be helping and adding value for the customers you serve, whilst making an incredible six-, seven- or even eight-figure income.

It's finally time for you to change your life, by giving value, helping others, and in return, making a fortune. Start thinking about your unique skills and talents, and how these will benefit others. Are you an expert at trading financial markets? Or perhaps you're skilled in the area of sales, marketing or product development? Or maybe you have knowledge when it comes to building businesses, real estate, fitness or weight loss, that you could share with others?

You'll be amazed at what people will pay to learn, and how much they'll pay to learn it from an expert who they like, trust and respect. I have seen people make millions of dollars selling everything from how to take pictures of birds or start a photography business, through to how to cut hair, start a barber shop or hair salon, or how to find winning products online and resell them at a profit. I've seen people develop their own products, too.

These educational offerings come in the form of online courses, online coaching – whether group or one-to-one – and in-person events or masterminds. Delivery is fast, efficient, fun and extremely profitable. It's common for the offers to be priced from between $2,500 and $10,000 for an online course on the low-end, to between $35,000 and $65,000 for a mastermind on the high-end.

You have full control over what you sell, what you charge, how much profit you make, and in what format you deliver the information. You can deliver it via a laptop, or in-person, at any location on Earth. You choose when you work, and how long you work for, and you select your employees, if you choose to have them, along with your close circle of talented, high-level friends.

In other words...

What: You choose it.
When: You choose it.
Where: You choose it.
With whom: You choose it.
These are the 4 Ws that together create an amazing business and an amazing life.

You are about to have the best job in the world

Whatever your niche, industry, knowledge or skill type, what you're about to learn in this book will work for you and allow you to create and sell your own information product, coaching service or agency offer, sharing either your unique knowledge or one of your skills, at a six-, seven- and even an eight-figure level; as I have achieved myself.

I have helped people of all ages, from all over the world, to do exactly that many times over. This works whether you'll be selling an online course, a mastermind, online group or one-to-one coaching, or running a services agency. This works in any sector, whether fitness, personal development, business building, or sales and marketing. Everything you need to build the business of your dreams, at an extremely profitable level, is waiting for you in this book.

Don't believe me? These are just a few of the people I've helped so far – my hope is that their stories will inspire you to achieve more than you thought possible.

I worked with a 21-year-old agency owner from Canada, who ran lead-generation campaigns for real estate companies. I took him from $18,000 per month to $54,000 per month – in just four months. I will share all the strategies I taught him later in this book.

I helped a 33-year-old fitness influencer from Dubai add over $500,000 per year to his income by creating a mastermind programme. When we started working together, he had a large social media following, but was not providing products, services or experiences outside of a $9 per-month phone app. I also guided him through building and selling an online course, which, when launched, will add over $1 million per year to his income.

Finally, I worked with a 45-year-old children's sports educator from Australia, taking him from $9,000 per month to $37,000 per month by helping him to better market and sell his online courses. I also helped him generate over $40,000 in cash in a single day using a re-offer (more on those later in the book).

Introduction

As you can see, what you'll learn in this book really can be applied whatever your age, location or industry.

You're about to learn how to create an offer so compelling that you'll have to turn people away because you have too many clients already. They'll be drawn to you because you'll be presenting them with a solution to such a severe and all-consuming problem that they'll be begging you to take their money in return for your new and unique antidote.

Then you'll learn how to package up and deliver that antidote in a simple, scalable and sustainable manner, so that your customers routinely achieve the result that they desire, and you consistently generate the income that you deserve.

From there, you'll learn how to take control over how many customers you choose to acquire, and at what cost, with what level of profit. You can, and will, finally have control over these critical business levers, so whether your aim is an income of $10,000 per month, $100,000 per month or even $1,000,000 per month, you can achieve it.

Finally, you'll learn how to systemise both your business and your life, so that you can regain your time, enjoy your income and live an incredible life of your own creation, on your own terms. You will have control, and you'll even be able to sell your business, if you so choose, like I did myself with my first online course and coaching company.

Are you ready to change your income, and your life, forever?

How to get the most from this book

In this book, I'll show you what to do and how to do it, when it comes to creating a thriving and highly profitable online business that will change both your life and the lives of your customers, but it will take work. I want you to commit to that work, and to gaining the knowledge you'll use to achieve that promised outcome, by reading this book in-full and as quickly as possible.

The mere fact that you're holding this book in your hands tells me that you believe in investing in yourself and your continued learning; that you want to share your knowledge and add value to others' lives; and that you aspire to building massive wealth and living life at its fullest, with total freedom and control. That means you have what it takes to succeed, so the only question then is, are you ready to dive in?

Let me say this, your time is now. By investing in this book, you've proven that to be true. I wrote this book for *you...*

If you dream of making millions of dollars doing something that you love, that fulfils you and that has a positive impact on others' lives...

If you want to share what you've learned, what you've mastered, what you're passionate about...

Introduction

If you want freedom, optionality and control...

If you want to build massive levels of wealth...

This book is for you.

P.S.

You'll benefit most from this book by reading it in order, cover to cover, rather than skipping around from section to section. I also strongly encourage you to keep a highlighter handy and mark what you find is most helpful and impactful for you, so that you can return to these highlights at a later date.

Chapter one

My Journey to an $850,000 Per Month Business

Hopefully you're excited about the prospect of taking control of your life and giving yourself the best job in the world. While that might all sound great, you might also be thinking: "W*hy should I listen to this guy?"*

It's a fair question. So, why should you listen to a word I have to say?

Simply put, when it comes to building something from scratch, on my own, with no investor capital, with absolutely zero skills or qualifications, and scaling it to multiple millions of dollars in income, I have been there and I have done it.

Yet I think it's fair to say that my journey has been unconventional...

Getting rolling as an entrepreneur

In my younger years, I did what many of us do – I got a job in a pub, washing glasses every Friday and Saturday night for $15 per night. I was 15 years old and it was far from glamorous, but it gave me all the money I needed at the time.

My only focus back then was high school and skateboarding with my friends, and the latter formed my first entrepreneurial venture. Me and my friends loved watching skateboard videos, but rather than just skateboard myself, I became inspired to create – and later sell – my own skateboard videos.

I saved up my pub money for a couple of months, bought a camera and some editing software and began filming. I didn't know it at the time, but my passion had led me to create my first-ever saleable product. I would produce the videos, make cover-art by-hand by cutting up magazines and newspapers to create collages, and I'd sell the copies to any other local skateboarders who wanted to watch them.

I did this purely for fun. It came naturally to me. The very small amount of money I made was simply a nice bonus. It was not my goal to "make money", and at this stage I did not know anything about business, let alone know what the word "entrepreneur" meant. I was just unleashing my inner creativity.

First entrepreneurial venture: *Skateboard videos*
All-time earnings: *2-figures*

As a by-product of skateboard culture, I stumbled into street art and graffiti a year or two later. This became my second substantial passion. I would write and paint graffiti with my friends, and we would read all of the graffiti books and magazines we could get our hands on.

This soon formed my second entrepreneurial venture – my own graffiti magazine. I'd learned to use Photoshop back when I made the covers for my skateboard videos, so I already had the basic skills needed to put pages, images, graphics and text together. Yet again, I began working on another product that I would soon be selling, this time in a slightly larger fashion.

I emailed famous graffiti artists to ask for interviews. I took the bus and the train up and down England to take pictures, and I slowly put together my first graffiti "zine" as we called them.

I was working at McDonald's part-time whilst studying art and media at college, earning about £200 ($360) per week. I saved this money and invested in professionally printing 100 copies of my first issue. I then delivered them by-hand to local boutique art and music shops on a sale-or-return basis, and as I travelled around England, I would sell them to other graffiti writers I would meet.

Second entrepreneurial venture: *Graffiti magazine*
All-time earnings: *4-figures*

Graffiti culture was not just about the art itself. Music was a huge component, and from city to city and country to country, the music that graffiti artists listened to ranged from punk and rock, to house and techno, to dubstep and drum and bass. I'm sure you can guess what happened next. In my late teens, I became obsessed with electronic music, particularly drum and bass, and later dubstep.

My love for graffiti slowly faded and my focus shifted to buying and playing music. This passion even inspired me to pursue a sound engineering degree at a university in Manchester.

Moving from the small northern town I'd grown up in to the city changed my life because it allowed me to attend the clubs that my favourite musicians were DJing at. I became immersed in the music I loved, further fuelling my passion to create my own music in the hopes that, one day, I'd hear my favourite artists playing my music in their sets.

I had hopes and dreams of becoming famous and touring the world, as my idols did. After two years of making my own music under the alias Compa, but getting no further than a few local DJ sets at small clubs and bars for zero income, I had an idea.

What if I self-pressed a one-off vinyl record with my music on it – which is called a "dubplate" in the underground music world – and I stood outside the club after one of my favourite artists had performed, in the hopes of catching them as they left, and handing them the record?

Most people at the time would email their music to record labels and artists, so giving out a physical vinyl record felt more unique and personal. I thought it would make me stand out and might make it more possible that my music would actually be heard, rather than lost in an email inbox.

It worked.

The genre of music I produced and played was dubstep, and the number one record label for the genre was called Deep Medi Musik, run by dubstep pioneer Mala. Every time he played in the city, I would be there. I was at the front of the crowd

as he played, and standing outside the club afterwards hoping I'd catch him as he left.

After a few failed attempts, I finally caught him one night leaving the Moho Live club in Manchester's Northern Quarter.

I spoke to him for a few minutes, gave him the dubplate, along with my email and phone number, and off he went.

Then, crickets.

I received no email. No phone call. Nothing. *Shit, my music is rubbish*, I thought. *I'm not good enough yet, I need to keep writing and producing.* I felt like a failure. My number one focus was getting signed to Deep Medi, but here I was, still working at McDonald's part-time whilst going through university, with next to no money. I mean this literally when I say that I only did three things, on repeat, for the entirety of my time in Manchester: Write music, go to university, attend dubstep shows.

My only success came in the form of a few unpaid gigs in Manchester and the surrounding areas. I got lucky here and there with a gig in London – playing the first set of the night, to nine people, unpaid I should add – and another in Leeds, but that was all that my success amounted to. Until...

Catching a break

Ten months after meeting Mala, I got a phone call from an unknown number. "Will, it's Mala, how are you man?" *Holy shit.* I was in the kitchen of my shared student house with my best friend Alex, and I had Mala on loud speaker. I was shaking with excitement. Mala told me he liked one of the tracks I had given him, but would I mind sending more music so that we could decide on an additional track to release? He wanted to put out a two-track single on Deep Medi.

I tried to play it cool, but it was the most exciting moment of my life. I quickly sent over all of the more recent music I'd been making. We chose a second track, and my first Deep Medi record was released.

Just weeks after signing to the label, with dubstep music booming at the time, I landed a booking agent and began touring the world almost immediately. My first-ever international bookings were in Amsterdam, Gothenburg and New York , and I was getting paid between $500 and $750 per performance with all expenses – flights, hotels, food and taxis – covered by each promoter who booked me. I could hardly believe it.

Suffice it to say, I quickly bid farewell to McDonald's and studying went out of the window, despite being in my final year of university at the time. I didn't drop out, but I did not care about the work. My dream was to be an international DJ and it had suddenly become a reality, taking me to over 40 countries around the world in 2012 and the years to come.

Third entrepreneurial venture: *Compa, music producer*
All-time earnings: *6-figures*

Music, when I was younger, was a thrilling career. I loved the travelling, the hotels, the clubs and festivals, the people I met, the performances – it was a dream come true. But I was an underground DJ and the most I was ever paid for a performance was $1,800 for a set at a festival in Istanbul, Turkey. On average, I was earning $2,500 per month and performing once per week, on either a Friday or a Saturday night.

After four or five years, the allure of travelling and performing began to fade and my love for creating music waned. My creativity had run dry and I was uninspired. Because I wasn't making music, only performing, DJ bookings got slower and slower. I had a realisation: do I want to be travelling like this and performing in clubs at 3am when I'm 40–50 years old? Absolutely not. If I was feeling lonely now, how would I feel if I had a wife and kids? Yet music was my only source of income and, at 25, I still lived with my parents.

But, I had an idea... What if I kept going and sustained my music career for as long as I could, penny-pinching and saving as much money as I could, to invest in a house? I could rent it out for $500 per month, do that two or three times, use the rental income to cover my living costs so that I break even, and then do music for fun again without needing to solely focus on creating an income from it.

It would take time, but it felt like a solid plan. I started saving as much as I could, and after about a year and a half, I had enough to buy my first rental property. It cost $51,000. I used a mortgage to buy it, putting 25 per cent of the purchase price down, spent a little more on a basic renovation, and I then rented it out for $550 per month. I still own that first house to this day, and as of me writing this, it's worth $95,000, so has almost doubled in value.

Fourth entrepreneurial venture: *Real estate investing*
All-time earnings: *7-figures*

At this moment in my story, I was 26. I had about $8,000 to my name, one investment property earning me an extra $550 per month, and I was earning an average of $2,500 per month performing as a musician. My ambition was to sustain

How to: $10M

performances, keep saving, keep slowly and steadily buying more real estate, and build wealth, albeit in an extremely uncertain career, whilst relying on nothing but hope.

Fast-forward five years though, and by age 31 I was a multi-millionaire, living in Dubai in an apartment overlooking the ocean earning, on average, $241,000 per month.

Yes, per month.

The big leap

How did I go from an electronic musician making on average $2,500 per month, to a multi-millionaire earning just shy of a quarter of a million per month? Pay very close attention as I explain the journey, because it happened in what felt like the flick of a switch, and it may for you, too.

It all started with mastering a high-value skill that, unbeknownst to me at the time, I would end up sharing with thousands of people around the world for a very favourable amount of money. One night after I returned home from a music performance in London, I came across a TV documentary on the subject of trading financial markets. I watched as I ate my dinner, and I was captivated.

It told the story of a handful of successful traders who, apparently, were making thousands trading from home. One of the subjects of the show was sharing their ability to make over $1,000 per day, from home, via nothing but a laptop. I was blown away. *Is this real?* was a question that came to mind. *Could I do it, too?* was another. I'm sure you can guess what happened next...

I ran to Google and searched "trading account", opened an account with the first broker I came across, threw $500 in and began trading. No strategy, no risk management, no real idea of what I was doing. Yet I became one of the lucky few who, through nothing but beginner's luck, made money quickly from day one. I grew the $500 up to almost $9,000 and felt like I'd mastered the markets. I was sure I was on track to make millions, and fast, until just a few weeks later when I wiped out half of the account on one trade.

Thousands disappeared in front of my eyes in seconds.

It was at that moment that I realised I didn't know what I was doing. I was gambling, and my luck had just run out. Everything I'd avoided considering quickly became clear to me – I had no strategy, no plan, no edge and no education. I was a sitting duck, and I had paid the price.

Filled with humiliation, regret and sadness, I stopped trading for weeks. I could not look at a stock chart. I was crushed. Yet in hindsight I realised making money as a trader was possible. After all, I'd made thousands before I'd lost it. It was in that moment of realisation that I made one of the best decisions of my life: I emptied the remainder of my trading account, leaving just $500 in there, and I set about investing the money I'd taken out on education.

I hired a coach, and then another, and then another. I bought online course after online course. Through months of study, practice, research, coaching and hard work, I was able to learn how to construct my own unique trading strategies that I used to slowly and consistently make money within my trading.

One day, a friend messaged me on Facebook after hearing from a mutual friend of ours about how well my trading was going. He offered to pay me $50, via PayPal, to come to my house and sit with me whilst I traded one morning. *Why not?* I thought, and invited him over, collecting the pay cheque.

Little did I know, a multi-million dollar e-learning company had just birthed itself organically.

During my friend's visit, we put together a three-page Word document that he could take away with him. A few days later, I started wondering if anyone else would buy the Word document for $50. So I took it upon myself to message a few friends and ask them. To my amazement, a small handful of them obliged, sent the money, and I manually emailed them the file.

I couldn't believe it. $50 for literally just sending over a Word document that I was paid to create in the first place. It truly felt like free money. A lightbulb went off in my mind... *I wonder if I could charge more if I made it better, adding images, more in-depth detail and so on; and imagine if I could sell it regularly, creating a second income?* My mind was firing with excitement at the idea. But how would I find the customers to buy it?

After some creative thinking, I decided to start a Twitter account and a YouTube channel sharing my thoughts and ideas in regards to trading, along with my live-trade recordings and commentary on the markets. My plan was to generate interest by sharing the content, start conversations with the people who followed me, and attempt to sell them the Word document.

It worked better than I ever could have imagined:

In my first year of selling the Word document, I made $28,438 in cash – £22,254 at today's exchange rate. I still have the earnings report to this day, which is pictured above. This was the start of a business that would go on to change mine and my family's lives forever, making me over $16,000,000 in the coming years.

As I kept increasing the quality of the education, I slowly and steadily raised the price in-line with the value I was providing, and the happiness and success of the customers I delivered the value to. The Word document turned into an ebook; then into a Dropbox folder of video content and explanatory documents; then into a full-blown online course; then into a training program featuring one-to-one coaching, group coaching, exercises to complete, documents to fill out and more.

Along the way, the price rose from $50, to $500, to $5,000 and alongside the growth of the product, I began hiring fantastic team members to help me with everything from customer support and coaching, to sales, advertising and marketing. At the time I sold the company, we had 16 members of staff and were tracking to make $4,500,000 that year in total sales revenue.

All from letting a friend pay me $50 via PayPal to come to my house for three hours.

Fifth entrepreneurial venture: *E-learning company*
All-time earnings: *8-figures*

The truth is, as crazy and inspiring as my story may sound, it is not an uncommon one. In fact, after reading this book, it is highly likely that the same will happen to you. You will either realise you have, or master, a high-value skill, and begin sharing it with others, creating a valuable offer in doing so. From there, you'll slowly iterate the offer and the price, going on to share it with hundreds or thousands of people worldwide, making millions of dollars in the process.

That's all it takes. Learn, or identify, a high-value skill or piece of knowledge or expertise that you possess. Package it up in the form of an online course, coaching program, event or mastermind. Attract interest from people who would benefit from learning the skill, knowledge or expertise, and sell it to them.

That might sound overly simplistic, but that is exactly how you will make millions of dollars in the coming months and years. This book will show you how to do it, step-by-step, leaving no stone unturned. Are you ready to become rich?

A new direction

You might be thinking, *Will, if you owned a business making hundreds of thousands of dollars per month, why did you sell it?* Good question. I chose to exit because I felt I had outgrown the vehicle I'd built. After removing myself from operations, my life became slow, uninspiring and I lacked purpose.

The money would roll in with little effort, and I would spend my days sleeping in with no alarm, going for lunch at the beach or coffee in the city, reading, meditating, going to the gym and occasionally checking my emails, looking over a tracking sheet or chatting with team members, but nothing more.

That might sound great, and it was for a few months, but it quickly became boring. I had already built a great product for our customers and, therefore, I had no further purpose-driven action to take. I'd run out of urgency to change people's lives or add value in the trading niche specifically, and I had no inspiration to build anything more of substance. All of which is, I realised, my true passion in life.

Which leads me to explain why I'm writing this book.

Around a year ago, one of my former mentors was sharing the story of my success during one of his mastermind events. An audience member Googled me, found my Instagram and messaged me asking for some ad-hoc coaching to help him build and scale his online education company in the e-commerce niche. We decided on a recurring monthly fee for one call per week, and I began sharing with him everything I'd learned in going from $0 to $16,400,000 in sales with my own e-learning company.

Three weeks in, he'd grown his company from $34,000 per month to $117,000 per month, and helping him achieve these results came naturally to me. I realised I had knowledge that many simply don't. Similar to how my online education company birthed itself organically, and almost as if history was repeating itself, I was taken over by a whole new energy, passion and focus.

I would get off the coaching calls feeling better, happier and more inspired than when I got on them. *This is it,* I realised. *This is what I'm supposed to do now.* So I began sharing what I'd learned with other smaller, newer and greener online business owners, helping them to dramatically grow their businesses – and I've never felt as driven, happy and inspired as I now do.

I feel like this is the start of the next chapter of my life. I want to share my energy, knowledge and passion for creating great products, selling them to those who need them, and adding value to others, with you in this book, along with exactly how you can start, or grow, your own online education business and quickly scale it to multiple millions of dollars in sales.

Read on, and I will not let you down.

Part one

The Core Building Blocks of an E-Learning Company

In this first part of the book, you will learn the core building blocks of an e-learning company. I want to show you just how easy it can be to build your own e-learning company, and I'll explain exactly how to do it step-by-step. There's a lot of "how" in here, I hold nothing back, but I want you to be inspired by what's possible, rather than overwhelmed by the steps.

As you read Part 1, you'll understand where to start, and what action to take once you've taken that all-important first step. In the coming eight chapters, I cover everything from how to work out who you help, to how to acquire customers and how to optimise your sales process.

I've also added real-world examples and even shared insights from some of the people I've helped to do this via my Build, Grow and Exit training programs, so that you can "see inside" other successful businesses and learn how others have done this themselves.

So, are you ready to lay the foundations for your wildly successful e-learning business?

Let's dive in.

Chapter 2

Defining Your Niche
and Ideal Client

The very first question you should be asking yourself before building anything, be that a product, an offer or your marketing assets, is: "Who, specifically, will I help, and how will I help them? What talent or skill or piece of knowledge can they benefit from, that I possess?"

Be as specific as possible because, as the saying goes, "the riches are in the niches". By asking this question and answering in specifics, you are essentially constructing your audience. They are the most important piece of the puzzle, because your audience are the people who will actually *buy* what you're about to start selling.

Step one, therefore, is defining your niche and who you will be helping through that niche. To show you just how specific you need to be, take a look at the following examples. These are all from people I have coached or know, either personally or through my network, and these online education businesses and agencies produce over $1,000,000 in annual sales. Some even produce over $1,000,000 per month. Yes, I said per month.

- How to run ads
- How to cut hair
- How to produce music
- How to get six-pack abs
- How to become a closer
- How to take pictures of birds

- How to stop drinking alcohol
- How to trade financial markets
- How to stop smoking cannabis
- How to generate qualified leads
- How to start a recruitment agency
- How to get a job selling software services
- How to talk to members of the opposite sex
- How to outsource the production of audiobooks
- How to start an accounting or bookkeeping business

Let me make this very clear – you almost certainly have a talent, skill or specific knowledge right now that you could package up and sell, whether as an online course, as a coaching program in a one-to-one or group setting online or in-person, as a live event or a mastermind, or as an agency.

But what if you don't currently have a talent, a skill or specific knowledge?

That's OK. You can learn one, *then* package it up.

Think back to my own story. I learned to trade, then I taught people how to trade. One of my personal friends learned how to conquer his alcohol addiction, then he taught people how to conquer their alcohol addiction. Another friend built a very successful recruitment agency, then he taught people how to build their own successful recruitment agencies, alongside running his agency.

Furthermore, another of my friends just last year took it upon herself to learn how to run Facebook lead generation ads by watching free tutorials on YouTube. She then started her own lead-generation agency, charging a $3,000 per-month retainer to run these ads for private dentists. After seeing great success, a couple of months ago she began teaching people how to start their own lead-generation agency for private health professionals such as dentists, doctors and physicians. She charges $5,000 for her coaching program and has made $35,000 selling it as of last time I saw her.

Are you starting to see how, even if you don't currently have a talent, a skill or specific knowledge – which you almost certainly do, you'd be amazed what people will pay to learn – you can always develop a talent, a skill or specific knowledge and *then* share it, just like I did?

You also don't need to be a breathtaking, one-of-a-kind master at what you teach. That's a common misconception. You simply need to be further ahead than those who you are teaching.

For example, let's say that you know how to make $1,000 per month selling items on eBay. Many people in the world would jump at the chance to learn how to make an extra $1,000 per month on the side. That's an extra $12,000 per year in income!

Now, is an extra $1,000 a month spectacular? For most people, it isn't, no. But could it change someone's life? In many cases, yes, absolutely. Therefore, the knowledge is very valuable and you could certainly charge $2,000 or $3,000 to share it. That upper price point would result in a 3x return on investment for the buyer across a year, creating a win-win value proposition.

That's what business is all about – creating win-win value propositions that help people.

The simplest way to articulate that value proposition is through an "I help" statement. So, right now, I want you to pick a talent, a skill or specific knowledge that you have. Write it down. If you can't think of one, then simply pick one from the list that I shared earlier in this chapter that you can work with for now. Next, let's develop your "I help" statement.

Dropping knowledge: how to write your "I help" statement

Your "I help" statement is a technique used to help you nail down exactly who, and how, you help people. Here's what an "I help" statement looks like:

I help [x] to [y] by [z].

For example:

I help losing traders to finally become profitable by sharing my unique mechanical trading strategies with them.

- I help struggling alcoholics to stop drinking alcohol by using first principles thinking.
- I help underpaid barbers learn how to build a personal brand, land high-profile clients and charge as high as $100 a haircut by sharing my star-cut methodology with them.
- I help avid readers to read up to three times as fast and retain twice as much information by sharing my proven, easy-to-learn speed-reading techniques.

So, who will you help? What will you help them to do? And how will you help them to do it?

When you have crafted your "I help" statement, you'll have a potent component of your soon-to-be marketing that you can put in your social media bio, or use to help you write your website or the written copy in your sales funnel – don't worry, we'll cover how to create these together later in the book – and more.

Your "I help" statement is the foundation of the business you'll create and build as you move through this book. It's the starting point that forms the building blocks of your company, and the value you'll be providing to the people you will soon be helping.

Don't worry if you can't think of one yet, sometimes just letting it sit in your subconscious is the right thing to do, and over the next few hours or days, it'll come to you as if by magic. For now, just ruminate on those three all-important questions:

1. Who will you help?

2. What will you help them to do?
3. How will you help them to do it?

A pain, a problem and a "push-button" solution

By writing your "I help" statement, you have identified the problem that you will solve for your audience. Now you need to make sure it's the right kind of problem, because the foundation of helping someone starts with their painful problem. If a problem is not painful, like a sore tooth aching to be pulled out, or a pounding, throbbing headache that just won't budge, then people will likely not pay much, if at all, to solve it.

I once heard this called a "bleeding neck" problem. Essentially, it is a problem so big that it just has to be solved immediately. Let's take this to the extreme. Imagine you had a knife stuck in your neck, you were bleeding out fast, your life was flashing in front of your eyes, you had just moments left to live... But standing in front of you was a person with a magical, instant cure that happened to cost $100. Would you pay that amount to stop the bleeding and prevent your death? I certainly would. How about if it cost $1,000 instead? Would you pay that to remain alive, or would you object and say, "That's too expensive!"?

Now let's raise the stakes and say that the magical, instant cure cost $10,000 instead and, for the sake of the example, you have this amount of money in the bank. Would you pay that to see your family and kids again, and to continue to live, or would you object and say, "Hmm, let me think about it", or, "I'm not sure, let me run it past my partner. Can we chat again tomorrow after I've slept on it?"

You see, objections usually come about as a result of either the person not seeing the value that you provide, or the problem not being big, hairy or painful enough to warrant investing in a solution. In some cases, the person may simply not understand how you can help them, or they may even be unaware that they have a problem that needs solving.

Objection handling is one of the key functions of your marketing and it all starts with your "I help" statement, which is why you must be as direct and specific as possible. When you nail this, you prevent people from being able to make excuses or find reasons *not* to buy.

There are two other things that are critical to the success of your offer, and your business. The first is making the solution as "push button" as possible, and the second is always keeping in mind the three pillars of pain, which we'll discuss shortly.

Finding your "push-button" solution

First, let's unpack the "push-button" solution. This is something I learned from one of my mentors, Alex Becker. He taught me that the easier the solution is to carry out, the more inclined a person will be to purchase your solution. He always stressed

the importance of making it as simple, fast, easy and "push button" as possible. For example, let's say you were selling an online course on the topic of creating ebooks and selling them online. What comes to mind for you, if you were to personally consider buying this course to teach you to create ebooks and sell them online? What would your biggest challenges to creating an ebook and selling it be?

Many people would say that they would struggle with writing a book, or creating the cover art. Others might say that they would get stuck on the technical setup, or the marketing or sales aspect of the project. There are obviously various stages to the process, but how might we make this "push button" for our customers?

One idea would be to hire an in-house writer to write the books for your customers. That's the first problem solved. We might also hire an in-house artist to create their cover art for them, thereby solving the second problem. Then we might build in-depth training content to go in the online course that explains the technical setup steps that need to be taken to sell an ebook online. That's the third problem solved. Finally, we might hire a professional marketer and an expert sales advisor to either do this for the customers, or hold a weekly group call on this subject to help them to do it themselves. Now we've solved the fourth and final problem too.

Can you see how we've just engineered the product to make it as easy and fast as possible for the customer to achieve the promised result? That's what I mean when I talk about a "push-button" solution. In this example, we've created a reliable, fast, easy way to create ebooks and sell them online, with little to no effort on the author's part, allowing them to quickly generate a new income stream.

"That's a pretty good offer. Where do I sign up?!"

The great news is you can take this approach for almost every product or service that it's possible to provide. The formula is simple: solve the hardships, remove the stumbling blocks, answer the questions or hire professionals to do so, and you'll soon have a product so great – so "push-button" – that it is a no-brainer of a purchase to make. This will allow you to easily make sales because, similar to what we discussed in our bleeding neck example earlier, you'll be presenting a solution to a pressing problem, in a "push-button" manner, and, therefore, be able to charge a high price point, potentially raking in millions over the coming months and years.

The three pillars of pain

So far we've explored how to make life easy for your customers, and we know the importance of solving a pressing problem – but how can you identify the most pressing problem among all the challenges your audience might face? That's where what I call the pillars of pain come in. These are the three core areas of human focus: health, wealth and relationships. Understanding these will help you to position your offer, product or service for greatest impact.

The pillars of health, wealth and relationships are the three biggest, most important areas of our lives as humans and it is a fact that we will pay money to ensure that we are great in one, if not all, of them. Hence, more often than not, the best offers to sell – namely the ones that sell the fastest and easiest, for the longest amount of time – fit into one of these three areas.

Think about your product and whether it can improve one of these areas. So, how can you improve someone's health? Or their level of income and wealth? Or their relationships with their family, friends or those of the opposite sex? Selling into one of these categories will make your life easier, and will make you money much faster and with less effort, because these are human fundamentals.

There are over 7.5 billion people on Earth, and we all want and need everything that comes with each of these pillars. We all want great health, abundant wealth and fantastic relationships, don't we? Or at the very least, we prioritise one if not two of the pillars, and then eventually the remaining pillar or pillars that we left unregulated grow in importance at a later stage in our lives. They are impossible to escape and only mount in importance if left unaddressed.

To tie everything we've just discussed together, and to make creating and selling your offer, product or service much easier, I strongly suggest thinking about what to create in terms of "wants versus needs", which is a technique I learned from one of my early business coaches.

Let me give you an example of selling wants versus selling needs. What people want is easy – stress-free, "push-button" results. They want to make money as quickly and easily as possible, without needing to master any specific knowledge or do any hard work. They want to get six-pack abs in one week, without needing to diet or exercise. They want to find the partner of their dreams, without needing to date or work on their personality or level of attractiveness. You get the picture.

Is it unrealistic? Yes, absolutely. Despite this, even knowing this, do people still *want* these things? Yes, they do. Let me present you with two offers, selling the same thing. One realistic, one unrealistic. Be honest with yourself, which of the following would you choose if they really existed and were possible?

1. "Lose 20 pounds in 16 weeks by exercising every single day, not being allowed to eat sugar or drink alcohol whatsoever, whilst also needing to fast for 24 hours one full day per week and only being allowed to eat 1,000 calories per day."
2. "Lose 20 pounds in just six weeks, guaranteed, using my new and unique 'rapid fat burn' weight-loss technique, without dieting, without going to the gym, and all whilst still enjoying all of the foods and drinks you love."

That's an extreme example, but I use it to convey my point. We all know that offer number one is the most realistic, and will almost certainly work – but most of us would not buy the offer because it requires effort, sacrifice and months of extremely hard work. Even if we did buy it, nine out of ten of us would not stick to it. Offer number two, on the other hand, is an extremely enticing offer. Results, without any hard work, without any effort and with little time expended.

Offer two is what we, and all humans, truly want. Therefore, it's our job, as product creators, service providers and coaches, to build an offer that is as close to option two as we can genuinely provide results and deliver on for our customers. It goes without saying that you should never sell something you cannot substantiate and provide. You will waste time, you will lose money and you may even get yourself into hot water from a legal perspective, too.

"Sell them what they want, but deliver them what they need," was something my business coach would often say when he taught me the "wants versus needs" offer creation technique. What he meant was that in order to make a lot of sales with much less difficulty, you cannot sell something like offer number one, and that you must get as close as you can to offer number two. But, and I can't stress this enough, you must deliver the promised result. The trick is making it sound easy, like offer number two, which is what the customer wants, while giving the customer the tools and knowledge they need to succeed with your online course or coaching program.

Your job is to make the effort, that's required, sound and feel as painless and effortless as possible for the customer.

How? A great way to do this is to start your online course or coaching program with two sections. The first is a mindset and understanding section where you instil the beliefs that your customer needs to have to achieve the promised result and do the necessary work. You might feature videos about self-belief, consistency, progress tracking, or whatever else is relevant to your specific offer. The second is a "copy-paste" section where you prepare done-for-you resources for your customers that remove as much hard work as possible for them. This could include sharing high-quality templates, ready-made documents, step-by-step setup videos, and so on.

As an example, when people join my business growth coaching program, I give them a "clone" of my own ready-built sales funnel that they can copy and paste with the click of a mouse, which saves them from needing to build their own. I also give them a copy of the exact sales script that me and my sales team used to sell over $10,000,000 of online courses within my e-learning company.

On top of that, I give them all of the tracking sheets, standard operating procedure documents, and files I used to scale my e-learning company. This saves them hours of time, removes a lot of hard work for them, and speeds up how quickly they get great results from working with me. I "blueprint" as many things as I can, and I deliver them in a "copy-paste" manner.

By doing so, I am hitting their wealth pillar of pain, because I am helping them grow their business, and, therefore, their wealth, quickly and efficiently. I'm also doing this in very much a "push-button" manner, removing days if not weeks of hard work for them.

The power of one per cent

By now, you should have pondered, or even decided on, who, specifically, you will help, and how you will help them. You should have been thinking about, or even written, your "I help" statement and you should understand the pain or the problem you'll be solving for the people you will be helping and serving. Ideally this is a pain or a problem that fits into one of the three pillars of pain, and your offer itself is built to sell what people want, in a way that you're able to deliver on and provide what they need to get results.

Before we move on and discuss how to find and attract the people you'll be helping through your offer, product or service, I want to share a concept that helped transform my own businesses, and those of the clients that I've coached. The concept is called "the power of one per cent".

This might sound strange, but most people will not buy from you, and that is OK. Whatever your offer, whatever product or service you provide, all you need is a tiny percentage of people who find out about it to buy at, let's say a price of $5,000. For many, just one or two high-ticket sales per month would change their financial life forever.

If you've ever worked in sales, you'll know that for every 100 leads, usually less than 30 will answer a cold call or respond to an email. For the 30 who do answer or respond, less than 10 will want to book in a full sales call thereafter. Of the few who do book in, it would not be uncommon for just one or two people to buy via the sales call itself.

100 leads → 30 answers → 8 sales calls → 2 sales at $5,000 each

That is very typical. My point being, 98 of those leads did not buy – whether they came from a social media following, paid advertising, an email list you bought, or otherwise.

Why am I telling you this? Because I want you to realise that your offer does not have to be for everyone, and it shouldn't be. In fact, in many cases, the more niche your offer is, the better it will sell because whilst the pool of buyers may be smaller, they will have much higher intent due to how much more they'll relate to it. Remember what I said earlier in this chapter – the riches are in the niches.

Some great questions to ask when creating an offer are why would someone *not* buy from me? What would turn them off? What would make their face screw up in disgust? What would send them running for the hills? As legendary entrepreneur Charlie Munger says, "Invert, always invert."[1]

1   Jennings, J. (2023) 'Remembering Charlie Munger: 5 of his most important pieces of advice,' *Forbes*, 29 November. https://www.forbes.com/sites/johnjennings/2023/11/29/charlie-munger-died-at-99here-are-his-5-most-important-pieces-of-advice/?sh=26622ec76b5c.

In other words, don't think "what do people want", instead think "what do people not want?" and then make sure to avoid these negative qualities. Think of it this way – by removing the reasons *not* to buy, the only choice is *to* buy.

Next, let's cover how and where to find, and attract, the people you'll be helping and serving.

Identifying your dream client

"Will, bro, I don't need 'dream' clients. I just need clients! Any client will do. I need sales!"

I hear you, and don't worry. We've all felt like that, but trust me, you do not want just *any* client. The wrong type of client will make your life a living hell. They'll badger you, call you, text you, email you and never leave you alone. They won't do the hard work required of them. They'll then complain and eventually ask for a refund and, like a cherry atop a cake, they will likely leave you a bad review, too.

We've all been there.

A dream client, however, will be a joy to work with. I am extremely careful who I allow into my private one-to-one business mentorship program because once you join, you can book in on my calendar for a one-to-one at any time you like, and you get my personal WhatsApp number, too. The people I let in are always awesome, focused, hard-working, dedicated and respect my time. The investment to get in is not small either, which in itself creates a lot of "buy-in" and commitment from those who I allow to work with me. These are fantastic, dream clients.

So, how do you find your own dream clients? The key is to understand them at a deep, deep level. You need to know their deepest desires, their fears, the things that keep them up at night sweating as they stare at the ceiling wishing things were different. You need to know their approximate age, their marital status, their job role and average income.

Deeper still, what happens throughout their average day on an hour-by-hour basis? What time do they wake up and go to bed? Do they walk or drive to work? What aspects of their life or personality affect how you market your product to them? What are they thinking when they see your ad or social media post or video, and what runs through their head and is the "deciding factor" in them pulling the trigger and buying from you?

This level of awareness runs deeper than the ocean. Knowing who you're selling to, and more specifically, the exact right person for your product or service, is the difference between making $25,000 a year and $25 million a year. That's not just a figure I've plucked from thin air by the way – I personally know three people who make over $25 million per year in total sales volume, and their businesses are built on this level of spectacular depth and detail.

Action points

Before moving onto the next chapter, I want you to pause here. Grab a pen and a piece of paper and bring together everything we've discussed so far. Write down who it is that you will help and how you will help them. Decide how you'll deliver your product or service – your offer – to them. Will it be via an online course, a one-to-one or a group coaching program (online or in-person), an in-person event or mastermind, or via an agency?

From there, write your "I help" statement and begin gaining a full understanding of the pain and the problem that you solve for the people you help, serve and add value for. Finally, answer all of the "ideal client" questions I shared and create three more questions of your own to help you fully and deeply understand your ideal client on your own.

Download William's 16.4M Dollar Resources

Scan the QR Code Below

Chapter 3

Acquiring Prospects – the Organic Route

Now that you've identified who your dream clients are, it's time to answer a few questions. Where are these dream clients exactly? How do you get their attention? And how do you get them to buy from you?

Before you can attract anyone's attention or get them to buy from you, you need to know where they reside online. If you help retirees, they're more likely to use Facebook than TikTok. If you help women, they're more likely to use Instagram than YouTube. If you help video editors, they're more likely to use YouTube than Facebook, and so on.

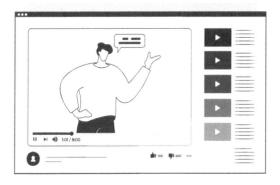

I also strongly suggest picking one platform and focusing on it. As one of my mentors Sam Ovens once explained to me: *"You only have so much focus. By spreading it across two things, instead of putting 100 per cent into one, you're now putting just 50 per cent into each. That causes damage, splits your focus and slows your progress down by half."*

As a tip for those who have not selected or made a start with a social media channel yet, I strongly suggest YouTube for most niches, because it is the only platform where content compounds on itself.

Think about it, when you post a YouTube video, it can only gain more and more views over time. On other platforms, however, this is not the case. Content gets seen when it's posted, and then it's slowly hidden and forgotten about as more content piles on top of it. YouTube is the only platform that allows your content to grow on its own over time, organically and for free.

Back to my own story; when I realised that there was a need in the marketplace for unique data-driven trading strategies, and that I could deliver on this need and provide the required solution, I started a Twitter account and a YouTube channel, with the intention of garnering interest from people who might have the problem that I knew I could solve.

The reason I picked Twitter is because it's the most common platform used by traders. The second most common platform used by traders is YouTube. Therefore, I started with Twitter first, I focused on building it and dialling it in for just over a year, and then I began a YouTube channel to further expand the audience I could reach.

Learning where your dream clients hang out is a pre-step to the following three-step process.

Step 1: Garner the attention of people who have the problem that you solve

Once I had my Twitter feed set up I would tweet inspiring quotes, share my trades, market-related ideas and theories, reply to other people's tweets who seemed like they may need help or be struggling, and share feedback from people I had already helped achieve great results. I would also do the same on my YouTube channel, posting videos of me trading and stories of my trading experiences, along with tips and tricks that would inspire people who may need my help, as well as interviews and testimonials from people I had already helped achieve great results.

Wow, not how

One thing I did not do, however, was share the "how". After all, if I shared that, they could solve their problem without me and would not need to buy from me. So instead, I gave them a "wow", showing them the trades, but keeping the strategies themselves hidden.

I wanted people to see my content and think, *wow, these strategies might be the answer to my struggles,* or *interesting, this guy seems to know something I don't, maybe I should ask for his help* and so on. The content was there to create likeability, trust and intrigue – essentially, to pre-sell people on buying from me.

The lesson is, never share your "how", only your "wow", whilst you garner interest from the people in your niche who have the problem that you offer a unique solution for. Share your story or how you solved the problem yourself. Share tips, tricks, ideas and inspiration to rile them up, get them excited and prove to them that you are the one who can help solve their "bleeding neck" problem. Post stories and testimonials from others you've helped, and whatever else you feel will add value – just always keep the "wow" not the "how" formula in mind.

Instagram, TikTok, Facebook, YouTube and X (formerly Twitter) are all great mediums for you to share content and begin building a following of people who you can help and add value for, using the "wow" not the "how" formula.

From there, I suggest creating your bio or description on your chosen platform that features your "I help" statement, along with a link to either your book-a-call calendar or your sales funnel. Don't worry, we will cover which to use and how to set both these options up shortly.

Step 2: Give those people a place to go to learn more, and to make a purchase

What we've just covered is called organic marketing. In other words, you're paying for attention using your time, by creating content and posting it, rather than paying for attention using your money, by running paid ads. Keep in mind though that the organic method is not free. You are paying with your time. In due course, and when the wheels of your education business are turning successfully and you're making sales, I strongly suggest moving to paid ads, which I'll cover in detail in the next chapter.

Let's continue with my own story to provide context to this.

In my first two years of selling my unique trading strategies to those who needed them, I marketed wholly organically via Twitter and YouTube. My only costs were my time spent creating content, and building on my product by improving the offering based on customer feedback.

But there was a limit on how much content I could pump out. I could not scale my business and reach more people because, as I learned and as I now often preach, you cannot control eyeballs. What I mean is, when you release a piece of organic content on social media, you cannot control how many people actually see it. However, you can control ad spend, which means when you run a paid ad on a social media platform, you can control how many people actually see it, by either spending less, or spending more. This gives you full control over how many leads or sales calls you buy, allowing you to control the scale of your business.

When you post a piece of content with the aim of generating organic leads, all you can do is "hope" that as many people as possible see it, and that some of them become interested in your help, and go on to make a purchase from you. Yet "hope" is not a viable business strategy. This is why, while I advocate for an organic approach to a point, you will at some point need to consider paid ads for client acquisition.

Now, can strictly organic traffic work at a low scale? Absolutely, and it does. You can make a great income via organic traffic only. I am an example of this – I initially grew my business up to roughly $45,000 per month using only my Twitter and my YouTube content for lead generation.

But I could not seem to scale past this mark.

The "you can't scale eyeballs, but you can scale ad spend" realisation was one presented to me by my first business mentor, Alex Becker, when I joined his mastermind – an $8,000 investment – as I headed into my third year of owning my e-learning company. Working with Alex changed my business and my life, and it taught me how critical it is to invest in knowledge and learn from those who've mastered the specific skills that you need to learn in order to continue to grow and progress.

After all, how can we expect people to buy *our* knowledge, if we don't invest in our *own* knowledge?

Alex taught me how to run YouTube ads, which made a huge difference to my business, incredibly quickly – and I'll come back to how and why in the next chapter. All you need to know for now is that organically growing your audience can be effective, but if you want to really scale your business, you'll need paid ads at some point.

Step 3: Pour fuel on the fire, and scale

Although ads are an important tactic to scale your reach, it's much better to use what you have rather than going straight for the money-spending option. This is why I advise anyone who already has an audience to use this first, then go to ads.

For those of you reading this book who are lucky enough to already have an audience – maybe you have an Instagram, X or TikTok account with 5,000 followers, a YouTube channel with 10,000 subscribers, or an email list containing 15,000 email addresses – you are in a fantastic position.

You will likely already have a brand and will have built up trust and respect with your followers. Maybe you're a fitness influencer, you run an educational e-commerce YouTube channel or Telegram group, or you're a musician with a loyal following. In any case, you should be very excited, as you can now make offers to your audience that, from my experience, will almost certainly result in immediate sales and revenue.

How? Because, usually, your audience has a clear problem, they follow you for help or guidance, and they are just waiting for you to offer a solution. When you do offer a solution to them, a portion of them – depending on the format i.e. online course, coaching, event or mastermind, and the price you decide to charge for the solution – will invariably lap it up.

Remember "the power of one per cent" that I mentioned earlier? As we discussed, all you need is for one per cent of your audience to buy from you, and you can make some serious income and begin adding value for those who would benefit from your knowledge and help.

Even if you only have, let's say 500 X followers, one per cent is five sales. Perhaps you have a larger audience of 1,000

Instagram followers. One per cent is 10 sales. Heck, even if just one person bought your program at a price of $3,000 each month, what impact would that have on your life?

Client story: Mike Thurston – fitness influencer

I'd like to introduce you to Mike Thurston, one of my business coaching clients...

I first met Mike during a dinner arranged by a mutual friend. At the dinner, I was talking to my friend about my upcoming business building mastermind that I host every six months at my home in Dubai. Mike, who was sitting next to me, asked, "What is a mastermind?"

I explained to him that it's an in-person event, usually limited to around 10 to 25 attendees, where a group of people meet up to share ideas, tips, tactics, strategies and knowledge centred around a specific subject, be that business, fitness, trading, personal development, meditation, writing and so on.

Mike then asked me, "Well, could I do one for my audience? And how would I structure it and sell it to them exactly?" I explained that, yes, absolutely he could, and said he should create and launch one, briefly explaining how. Off the back of that conversation, Mike joined my business coaching program, where I work with clients one-to-one over Zoom to help them build their offer and sales process, properly

price it, and then take the offer to market and sell it – don't worry, we'll cover all of this together later in the book.

What happened next? After just three weeks and three one-to-one calls with me, Mike and I had built his mastermind and event structure, created a sales video for his YouTube channel and decided on pricing. It was time to take the offer to market, so we uploaded the sales video to his channel.

Within just 48 hours, he had sold all 15 of the tickets that were available at $10,000 each, making well over $100,000 in total sales. He later told me that he couldn't believe that amount of money was sitting there within his audience, and that all he'd needed was the knowledge to unlock it. The answer for Mike, and the most valuable solution for his audience was a mastermind event, but he is currently building an online course, launching soon.

Since then, Mike has hosted three masterminds, and he has made around $325,000 in the process. Who knows, if we hadn't met at that dinner that fateful night, that money would likely still be sitting there, waiting to be picked up. For those of you who currently have an audience of whatever size, let me ask you, how much money is sitting there waiting to be collected by you, when you create an offer that provides huge value for your followers, and solves one, or more, of their problems?

The problem that Mike's audience had was as follows: they wanted to understand how Mike lives his life, which they see as the "dream" life. They wanted to learn how he produces content and how he has grown such a large audience. They wanted to experience Mike's gym routine, his diet, nutrition and so on. We solved these problems by allowing attendees to spend a weekend with him, seeing inside all of these areas of his life and business.

Sell before build

At this point, some of you may be thinking, *Right, time to build an online course to sell, right?* Wrong. Never, ever build a product and then try to sell it. People who do this see their businesses die and get buried in the graveyard of failed product ideas. After all, we might think our product is amazing, but who makes that decision?

Customers do, not us as creators.

This is why it's critical – no, essential – to sell before you build. And if you're thinking, *But Will, if I make a sale, they'll see that there is no product and surely they'll freak out and ask for a refund, won't they?* Don't panic. Here's exactly how to do this correctly, for explosive growth, immediate income, and in order to create an amazing product that will add massive value for your clients.

Step 1: Write a post, or release a video or piece of content, or launch a paid ad, making an offer to your market (I'll explain how shortly).

Step 2: Book sales calls, or start conversations, with anyone who is interested in your offer or help.

Step 3: When closing them on the sales call, tell them the following...

> "Currently [first name] I'm building the [product, event or mastermind] and as one of the first people to join, I'll be giving you and the other first-in clients not only a discount on the official launch-price, but also complimentary one-to-one coaching with me as I build the [product, event or mastermind] with you and the others in real-time.
>
> I'm doing this because I want to make sure that the [product, event or mastermind] content is exactly what you need to

[get results or solve problems] and whatever you need is in there for you, including the videos, resources, work-sheets, everything. It's all going to be built around you, and more importantly, your success and results. Sound good?"

From there, you collect the payment, decide on the day and time each week that you'll have a group video call with the members, and begin sharing all of the value you have with them in order to get them the result or the outcome that your offer promises to deliver. As you coach them, you'll keep notes on what works and what doesn't. Later, you'll turn that into version one of your online course or coaching program with full confidence in it being perfect, based on your test group and their success.

And better yet, the money is in the bank before you've built a thing!

Let me add one caveat; I understand that some courses or coaching programs can't be delivered live. If this is the case for you, I suggest building a "minimum viable product" that's simple, basic and just good enough to get your first batch of five or ten customers the promised result. However, do not waste your time attempting to build what you believe to be a spectacular product before the market approves it and people vote with their wallets by investing in it. Only once you have market approval should you build version one – or two – of your product, program or service.

Typically, if you work hard and fast after reading this book in full, you can have an offer crafted, posts made or ads running, sales calls booked and a sale or two closed in four or five weeks. Whenever I work with people via my business coaching program, even complete newbies, we often achieve this. If you want to go a little slower, that's OK. I encourage you to shoot for having at least one sale made within eight weeks of either reading this book in full, or joining me as a coaching client.

We'll go deeper on this in Chapter 8 when we talk about servicing your clients. This is when I'll walk you through the exact steps, strategies, timelines and more for building a great product or service.

How to write posts that make you $1,000,000

Now that you know that you don't need to build your product before you start selling, it's time to attract some attention. In doing so, you can book some sales calls, or start some conversations with prospective buyers – also known as prospects – and make your first few sales.

Client story: Alex Alleyne – sales professional

At this point I'd like you to meet another of my business coaching clients, Alex Alleyne. Alex found me via my YouTube channel – remember how I told you how powerful YouTube is as a channel for attracting prospects? – and he got in touch to ask for my help in building an online course centred around teaching people how to begin a career in software sales, which he had superior knowledge and experience in himself.

Alex was in the lucky position of having a small, but solid LinkedIn following, with many of his followers being low-paid sales people, in jobs that they either disliked at best, or hated at worst. These people either did not know how lucrative software sales is, or if they did know, they were not aware of how to get a high-paying role in software sales and were scared of making the jump from their existing role.

Golden handcuffs is the term to describe this – someone who is making decent money in their current job, but who wants more. However, they're scared to make the jump in case it doesn't work out. Alex wanted to solve this problem by offering to educate them on exactly how to quickly and easily land a high-paying software sales role.

So, we set out on a path of "sell-before-build" by writing some call-to-action posts for his LinkedIn account to encourage his followers to book sales calls. The idea was Alex would then pre-sell his £8,000 ($10,000) coaching program. We chose this price because we knew that Alex's successful students would make this amount back in only three or four months of work, and we also knew that his followers were in a "good" financial position already, and could, therefore, afford to invest this in themselves if they truly believed Alex could help them.

After only three weeks of working with Alex, and only two one-to-one calls together, out went the first post. The results were phenomenal – Alex saw a huge 20 qualified sales calls appear on his calendar. If you're scared of sales by the way, keep reading as I'll teach you how easy it is, and how to conduct and close calls later in the book. From these calls, Alex immediately started making sales.

After just a couple of days and within his first few calls, Alex had already made two sales, adding just shy of $20,000 to his bank balance, and welcoming two clients into his coaching program. He followed the sell-before-build methodology and arranged a weekly group coaching call, hosted via Zoom, with his clients in order to begin helping them, adding value for them, and getting them the promised result.

It really is that easy. As in both Mike Thurston's and Alex Alleyne's cases, the money was just sitting there waiting to be picked up. And if you're thinking, *But Will, they both had existing audiences. I do not have an audience at all. How can I get started and sell the offer I've created?* Fear not. It really is as easy as creating some content, putting it out there, and communicating with the people you begin to reach. It may take a few weeks to begin to build up your audience, but have patience because I assure you, that patience will pay off.

To see how it's done, let's take a look at one of Alex's early LinkedIn posts:

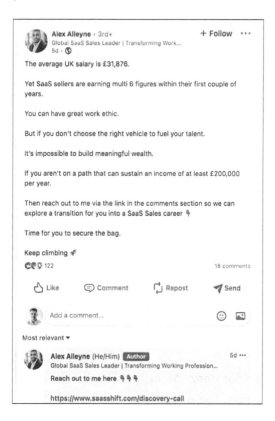

As you can see, it is short, simple and has a strong call to action, which is the thing that you want your followers to do. That might be book a call, comment below, click the like button and expect a message from me or fill out this form. You get the picture. Whatever you want them to do, don't just hope that they do it. Tell them precisely what to do, when, where and why.

The nine-word email

The next technique for building your audience that I'd like to share is the nine-word email. Invented by legendary copywriter Dean Jackson, the nine-word email is an extremely simple, call-to-action based post, that you can send as an email, or use as a social media post. It's effective due to its brief nature. It gets straight to the point – no fluff, just call out the problem, deliver the call to action, that's it. Side note: it also does not need to be nine words in length, that's just what the technique is called.

Here's one I used to love using to book sales calls for my e-learning company:

> "Hi [first name],
>
> Do you still need help with your trading? Hit reply and let me know."

I had an appointment setter who would contact everyone who replied, asking for their number and then giving them a call to have a chat to discover if we could help them. If we found that we could, the appointment setter would book them in for a sales call, they'd speak to a sales rep and join our coaching program.

Here's another post that worked well for us:

> "Hi [first name], we're looking for new clients to join the freshly updated version of our coaching program, where you'll learn our unique mechanical trading strategies, along with receiving professional-level coaching to up your trading game. Would that help you? Hit reply and let me know."

Again, an appointment setter would take it from there.

Dropping knowledge: how to write your nine-word email

These posts are so easy and fun to create. Here's a template you can use.

"Hey [name]. Do you still need help with [problem]? [call to action] and I'll lend a hand."

As a caveat, just because this style of post was invented for email by Dean, that does not mean you can only use it via email. It can also be used to create posts that you can then share on your Instagram story, your YouTube channel in the "posts" section, your X, your Facebook timeline or page, and so on.

You can put these short, catchy call-to-action posts anywhere that your audience is watching – just like Alex Alleyne did to make his first five-figures in cash in less than a month. Get their attention, call out their problem, provide them with a call-to-action and just watch the responses flood in.

Better still, as your audience grows in size, the responses will grow in size, too. From there, you can get people on a sales call, or just chat to them via direct message, move through the script that I will give you later in this book, and close them into your course, coaching program, event or mastermind.

It really is that simple.

How to master cold outreach

When it comes to prospects, they are either cold, warm or hot.

Working backwards, a hot prospect is someone who knows you, likes you, trusts you and if given the chance, would love to buy from you. All they need is a prompt to do so, and as long as they have the problem that your product solves, they will buy with next to no resistance.

A warm prospect is someone who may be following you, but who might not know exactly what you do or if you can help them. Usually, influencer audiences and celebrity audiences are, for the most part, considered warm. They are not red-hot raving fans who are itching to give away their money quite yet, but when provided with value and a strong call to action that creates intrigue, they will quite easily book a sales call.

A cold prospect is someone who is, well, stone cold. They either barely know of you, or they do not know you whatsoever. Thus, they have no idea what you do or how you can help them, and due to this, they do not trust you yet either. But don't let this scare you, as cold outreach and warm outreach are two of the most effective ways to generate interest in your offer and book sales calls.

What's the difference? Let me give you three scenarios...

Scenario one – My client Alex Alleyne identified people on LinkedIn, who he felt he could help transition into an SaaS sales role through his offer, by looking at their job titles. This is cold outreach because he did not know them and they did not know him. He used more of a creative message to spur them into action:

> "Hey [name], I see you're in [job role] at the moment. I've heard it's been tricky for the industry this year. I read an article on [something they'd relate to about the career itself, that may also trigger pain at remaining in the role]. How's it all going in [career type]?"

From there, if they replied, he'd introduce his unique mechanism. He would mention how high-paid SaaS sales roles are and how easy they are to transition into. Then he'd attempt to get them on a discovery call. This cold outreach method got him his first ever $10,000 "full-pay" sale, whereby the customer paid in full. Alex achieved that within just seven cold messages sent in a single day, no less.

Scenario two – Another of my clients, Cameron Heyes, did not need to go immediately to cold outreach and instead used warm outreach to book sales calls. He had a virtual assistant message his Instagram and Twitter followers with a slightly more relaxed and open message:

> "Hey it's Josh from Cam's team, he asked me to reach out to a few followers to see if any of his audience would like to test-drive his new 'x' program. Just to check [name], would you be interested at all? Absolutely no worries if not. Let me know."

From there, if they replied, Cameron had his virtual assistant send them a link to a page with a short, to-the-point sales video and a "book a call" button just beneath it. The video explained his offer, the value it provided, the problem it solved and so on. The prospects who resonated with this were able to simply book a call, fill out a survey for qualification purposes and speak to Cameron regarding the offer. He was then able to close them straight into his program.

Scenario three – Another client of mine, Alex Tharby, went straight to cold outreach. No fucks given. He set about sending short, sharp Loom videos to people on LinkedIn to start a conversation with the intention of booking calls for his agency in order to sell his lead-generation offer. He also sent the Loom videos to the Instagram followers of high-profile leaders in his industry, as he knew these people would likely resonate with his message.

Full transparency, he was only booking around three calls for every 100 Loom videos that he sent out, and, of those, only one or two would show up. So he had to grind hard. But he was sending over 200+ Loom videos per day. These led to a handful of calls each week, inevitably leading him to close his first client inside of two weeks on a $3,000 per month retainer.

Both cold and warm outreach are fantastic ways to book calls and close sales.

Action points

I know you're itching to learn more about how to use paid ads to scale your reach and your business, but pause for a moment before you move on. Get your pen and paper out and write down which platform (or platforms if you want to use YouTube plus another social media platform) you're most likely to find your dream clients on.

Next, follow the three steps I've outlined in this chapter to write a series of posts, or some content, designed to garner attention from these dream clients along with giving them somewhere to go to learn more or make a purchase from you. Then decide which of the techniques I've just detailed – the

nine-word email, warm outreach or cold outreach – you plan to use to pour fuel on that fire and scale up.

Remember, it's always best to sell first to a small number of people – three, five or ten – and then build your product later when you fully understand what they want and need, based on the feedback you gather by teaching them live.

Chapter 4

Acquiring Prospects – the Paid Route

As I mentioned in the last chapter, I was able to effectively grow my audience organically, but turning on paid ads was what allowed me to scale incredibly quickly – it was like pouring fuel on a fire.

The year I turned ads on, my business quadrupled, going from roughly $285,000 the year prior, right up to $1,300,000 that year. The growth was instant and explosive. I turned paid ads on in January of 2020 and immediately saw a month-one 10.3x cash return on investment – for every $1 I was spending, I made $10.30 back in profit, inside of the month itself. At the time, I did not understand just how phenomenal this return on investment was. I was new to paid ads and thought it was normal.

I launched my first YouTube ads just 11 days after joining Alex Becker's mastermind in December 2019. Just 12 days prior, I did not know what a "sales funnel" was or how to write or create a YouTube ad. I did not know what an "auto-webinar" was, how to write one, or how to properly price my product. I knew next to nothing.

I devoured Alex's training material and spent 12 hours per day learning and building. Just under two weeks after investing $8,000 in Alex's mastermind, I turned on my first-ever ads into the first funnel I'd ever built, and began making a 1,000%+ monthly return on ad spend out of the gate.

You can see in the image above, I spent a tiny £408 ($522) in my first month and made £4,227 ($5,410) in net profit, with an ROI of 10.3x cash. The following months, I slowly began to turn my ad spend up. One of my biggest regrets is not scaling faster.

Nonetheless, I slowly raised my advertising spend. From $25 per day, to $250 per day, to $2,500 per day across the coming months and years. When I sold my business, we were spending a very large amount on paid ads to fuel growth – approximately $6,000 per day.

If that amount scares you, that's OK. It would have scared me too, back when I was new to paid advertising and only spending a few hundred per month. But let me assure you, the minute that you are spending $1 on ads and getting anything more than $2 back inside of the month, then you should scale.

Spend more because, in most cases, growth is that simple.

How to write ads that make you $1,000,000

What if you don't have an audience? What if you don't want to build one? What if you have an audience, and you want to run ads to them via retargeting, which means only showing ads to people who have seen or engaged with your content already?

Or how about if you just want to straight up run paid ads to everyday people right away – the cold traffic I talked about in the last chapter? In this situation your aim is to put your offer in front of them and drive them into a calendar, sales funnel, written sales page or something similar.

Paid advertising gives you control over gaining as much, or as little, attention as you like. You can spend $10 per day, $10,000 per day, or more. This then allows you to convert that attention into sales. How? The first is by targeting specific audience segments using things like keywords i.e. "get a six pack", "trading strategies", or "how to stop drinking alcohol". The second is by retargeting your existing audience, whatever platform they're on, and then sending those highly-targeted people into your sales process, where they'll find more

information on what you do, who you are and how you can help them.

Here's how it looks, step-by-step:

Step 1: Get traffic – organic or paid.

Step 2: Sales process – a written page, order form, funnel opt-in, or calendar to book a call.

Step 3: Give a call to action – book a call, begin a conversation via direct message, or purchase.

Step 4: Close the sale – close the sales call or the conversation via message, or receive the purchase.

Don't worry, we'll dive deeper into the different types of sales process soon. For now, let's stick with the topic of paid ads. As a next step, let me share an amazing formula for writing advertising copy. This is a formula I learned from my early mentor Alex Becker when I was in his mastermind.

Dropping knowledge: a formula for YouTube ad success

0 to 10 seconds	Hook or con to not watching.
10 to 60 seconds	Promise/explanation/the how/ testimonials/call to action.
60 to 120 seconds	Benefits/without this thing/results.
120 seconds onward	Testimonials/call to action/ end screen.

Pro tip: Never end your ad without running some testimonials for up to 15 seconds afterwards, to let people digest the ad and click the link before it shuts off. If your ad suddenly ends and they are thrown back into watching the TikTok or YouTube video that they were watching, they will quickly forget about you, your ad, and the website you just mentioned.

Let's unpack some of those phrases from this formula.

A hook is something that grabs someone by the throat and forces them to pay attention.

"Why are you still   money within your trading?" is a hook that has done amazingly well for my e-learning company.

"Is your wife cheating on you as we speak?" is a hook that I saw do incredibly well via a dating offer.

"You'll be dead in as soon as a year from now if you don't stop drinking alcohol immediately" is a further example of a successful hook from an addiction offer.

A hook is there to do two things. One, attract your ideal prospect. Two, repel anyone who is not your ideal prospect. Next let's cover the alternative, which is the con to not watching. This is simply another type of hook, but usually focused explicitly on a key pain point.

"If you skip this ad, you will only carry on losing money within your trading," is one example.

"You can skip this ad if you like, but it'll be another six months before you find out your wife is cheating on you," is another.

"Is this why your e-commerce products never seem to sell? I'll share the solution with you in the next 30 seconds," is yet another.

These are designed to grab your ideal prospect and trigger immediate pain, fear and intrigue, in order to keep them glued to the ad as we explain how we can help and add value for the viewer. This brings us to the promise, which is simply how, specifically, we can solve a problem, relieve a pain or deliver an outcome for someone who becomes one of our clients.

"Stay with me for the next 60 seconds and I'll show you exactly how you can have your children sleeping soundly right through the night, in as soon as 24 hours from now," is an example of a promise that might be used in a parental consulting offer.

Can you see how we've only asked for a small time commitment in order for the viewer to feel comfortable paying attention? We've also made a strong promise that will attract exactly the right people – namely people with children who constantly wake up through the night, damaging your sleep and maybe even your relationship – whilst repelling the wrong ones, people without children.

"In the next 45 seconds, I'm going to show you how to gain the freedom and lifestyle of a six to seven figure recruitment agency owner" is an example of a promise that a friend of mine used in his most successful ad within his consulting company where he helps people to start or grow their own recruitment agency.

Again, he's used the "small time commitment" angle here, and his promise is gain-based, rather than pain-based. He helps people to "gain" freedom and an amazing lifestyle, much like the one he's created for himself.

Next, let's unpack the explanation, how, and examples part of your ad. This is simply when you explain how your offer works, how you can help the person, and share examples, usually in the form of testimonials from people you've already helped.

Don't worry, if you don't yet have testimonials. None of us start out with them, we all have to earn them. Not having them will *not* stop your ads from working, or your offer from selling. Think back to the "sell before build" strategy I shared in the last chapter. Just be honest with people, lean on your past successes or accolades as proof that you can do what you say you can, and use the fact that your offer is new as a way to make sales by offering a discount and complimentary group coaching until you have both a great, well-built program and testimonials from your early-access clients.

"If you've never heard of mechanical trading strategies before, don't worry, they are new to most people. They are built using statistical data, which proves that they work, which gives peace of mind and ensures that you'll get results. Take Amanda for example, she…" is an example of the explanation-how-example section of an ad.

95

"If you've tried and failed to stop drinking for years, did you know that by using first-principles thinking, you can rewire your brain to be disgusted by alcohol, as soon as today? It works by providing new mental model architecture for your neural pathways, and don't worry, it's completely safe and is backed by scientific data. Take Steven for example, he…" is another example of the explanation-how-example section of an ad.

See, writing ads is easy. And fun! From there, we just add in a call to action.

"If you'd like to learn more, click the button on this ad, and it'll take you to a short free training course I've put together that explains x, y and z in-detail. You can even book a free coaching call with me…" is one example of a simple, straight-forward call to action.

"Look, I can't explain everything in this short ad, but if you click the button on the ad itself, you can sign up for a free webinar I'm holding this week where we will take a deep-dive into exactly how x, y and z work, both in theory and in practice, too. You'll even have the chance to book a free coaching call with me…" is another example of a simple, straight-forward call to action.

Don't worry, I haven't forgotten to go through the benefits/ without this thing/results step – you'll want two calls to action in your ad, and that's just the first one. This next part of an ad is for people who have not yet clicked the link on the ad and taken the action we've asked them to take – basically they may need a little more convincing.

> "See, the major benefit to mechanical trading is that it removes emotion and guesswork. More than that, you do not need to do any complex analysis or spend hours at the charts. Take Melissa for example...".

See what I did there? I gave them a clear benefit, then I explained that the usual hardships are not involved and the usual stuff that holds them up is something they'll never have to worry about again. From there, I then rolled into another client example to back up my claims and share a result achieved by someone who's bought the offer in the past, and got a great outcome.

> "When you own your own recruitment agency, you'll be able to work as little as two hours per day, treat your spouse to that brand new shiny car, and you'll do it all without having to go to a physical office, without being called up at 3am by a troublesome client, and whilst earning high five figures per month, just like my client Andrew...".

Same again. I've shared two benefits that an ideal client would love to achieve, then I've removed their worries or the key things that they either hate, or that would worry them about proceeding with a recruitment agency, and I've then wrapped those claims and promises in a client testimonial to provide both proof, and a tangible result to calm their scepticism, if there is any.

After that, we simply roll into our second and final call to action, and we have a finished ad. Your second call to action can be very similar to your first, so you don't need to reinvent the wheel – just make it simple and compelling for the prospect to take action.

A word of advice: do not use sales language

One thing to keep in mind is to stay away from sales language, especially in your call to action, or you will cause what's known as "sales resistance" whereby people resist taking action, because they hate to be sold to.

So, rather than "sales call", instead you would say "complementary strategy session" or "free coaching call". You would not say, "Click the link and go and watch my sales presentation where I'll attempt to convince you to buy something," you would instead say, "Click the link and you'll find an exclusive free training I've prepared for you, where I'll share more info on 'x' to help you understand if it's right for you or not."

But Will, is that not lying to the viewer?

It isn't, no. It is simply reframing the value we're sharing with them. We all know that an ad is a paid-for commercial, created to drive sales. But if done tastefully and respectfully, and if the ad is there to promote a product, offer or service that truly helps people and adds value, then that's a great thing. In my opinion, if you have a skill, a talent or a unique piece of knowledge that will benefit the world, you should be doing anything and everything you can to get it into the hands of people who need it.

What they want, with none of the things they hate

At this stage, it's time to develop our persuasion skills via an additional piece of guidance I learned from one of my mentors regarding writing influential advertising and marketing copy. When writing your ads, keep in mind two key things:

1. What a prospective buyer wants.
2. What they strongly dislike, or even hate.

Let's come back to my earlier example regarding the ebook offer. Do you remember all of those stumbling blocks that we removed in order to make the offer a no-brainer? Let me remind you; pretend you are selling an online course on the topic of teaching people how to create their own ebooks and then sell them online.

Some people faced with the business proposition of creating ebooks, and selling them online, might say that they'll struggle with writing a book, or creating the cover-art. Others might say that they'll get stuck on the technical setup, or the marketing or sales aspect of the book, right?

Let's list these obstacles:

- I will struggle to write a book.
- I don't know how to design cover art.

- I have no idea how to sell ebooks or how to do any techy stuff.
- I don't know a thing about sales, advertising or marketing. How will I get them out there?

My point is this – the above offer is far from a "push-button" solution. What people *want* is to make money as quickly and as easily as possible. What people *hate* is hard work, or complex and time-consuming tasks. We must keep this in mind when building our ads, or any written copy or sales material. As Alex Becker taught me, "Sell people what they want, without any of the things they hate." In other words, "Sell them what they want, but provide them with what they need." We might be in a strong position to solve our prospects' problems with our program, but how do we show them this in our sales and marketing?

How do we do this within the program itself?

As mentioned earlier, we could hire an in-house writer to write the books for our customers. We might also hire an in-house artist to create their cover-art for them. Then we might build in-depth training content to go in the online course that explains the exact technical setup steps that need to be taken. Finally, we might hire a professional marketer and an expert sales advisor to either do this for the customers, or hold a weekly group call on this subject to help them to do it themselves. Now we've solved all four of the objections listed earlier.

How do we do this in our sales and marketing?

Let me share an example of a real-life, high-performing ad with you. What follows is the word-by-word script behind my best performing ad of all time. This is an ad that, by itself, has made me over $1,000,000 in profit, and that has racked up YouTube views of well into the multiple millions.

Let's break it down together:

> "If you're losing money as a trader, here's why: Emotion. That's the problem. See, …"

This is a strong and unique "hook" that calls out our ideal prospect: someone who is losing money within their trading – which is their painful problem – and who is mindful of the fact that they are trading using emotion. Our product solves both problems – it stops them losing money and removes emotion. We've achieved this literally three seconds into the advert.

> "Paul Tudor Jones is one of the greatest traders that ever lived. The strategy he used? He used market statistics, as shown in this documentary made about him, to put rules in place that he then used to inform his decision-making and the trades he placed.
>
> He wasn't using emotion or best-guess based things like trend lines or support or resistance, or anything else you've

likely learned in the past. He used a set of predetermined mechanical rules. Zero emotion. Again, set of rules.

George Soros, another of the greatest traders that ever lived. The strategy he used? He built macro-economic outlooks using, you guessed it, statistics as he explains in this interview, and he then used these to put rules in place that he then used to inform his decision-making and the trades he placed.

He wasn't using hob-nob indicators like an RSI or a Bollinger Band or a MACD, or anything else you've likely learned in the past. He used a set of predetermined mechanical rules. Zero emotion. Again, set of rules."

By this stage, we have tied our solution – mechanical trading rules – to two of the world's greatest traders, subtly pairing their success with what our prospects want to achieve. We've also highlighted the common losing techniques – trend lines, indicators, RSIs and so on – separating them from our new, unique method. In doing so, we're positioning our solution, mechanical trading rules, as "the thing they've never heard of, and never yet tried" with the intention of causing our prospects to think, *maybe this is the answer, the thing I've been missing all along, that finally turns my trading around.*

"That's all they did to succeed: They built mechanical rules, and they followed them. That's the secret. And it's one almost no traders know about. In fact, maybe you've never heard of trading using mechanical rules either, which proves my point."

We're walking deep into the psychological persuasion trenches here, but notice how I say words like "secret" and add in phrases like "maybe you've never heard of them, which proves my point" with the intention of making viewers think, *wow, that's why I've never heard of them before.*

"And if that's the case, I'm actually holding a free training workshop at the moment where I literally walk you through a set of mechanical rules along with explaining how they actually work. Just click this ad, either top-right if you're on mobile or bottom-left if you're on desktop, and they're waiting for you on the next page, whatever your trading platform, whatever country you're in, whether you're a new or experienced trader. Because the rules are statistically-proven, because they're built in advance of trading them, your only job is: Learn them, follow them and make money. It's that simple."

I've now thrown three key aspects of a successful ad in here. Can you spot them? One is adding a call to action, the second is using non-sales language by positioning the sales video as a "free training" and the third is using Alex Becker's what they want, with none of the things they hate technique by saying, "Your only job is to learn them, follow them and make money."

In other words, there's no heavy lifting and no techy stuff involved. Whatever your trading platform, whatever country you're in, whether you're new or experienced, this will work for you. We've also added in what people want – easy, push-button, minimal work, just follow the rules and make money – whilst removing what people hate – hard work, complexity, techy stuff, moving trading platform, sales language and so on.

"And if you're thinking, 'Yeah right, if only a set of rules that I could just follow to pull money out of the markets existed' well, …

Take Steve. This guy was flooding his charts with indicators, so much so he just didn't know when, or where, to get in or out of the markets effectively. I then handed him a set of mechanical rules and literally day two of using them he pulled £1,796 out of the markets with zero thought or stress or emotion, just by following them. And he was so happy, so shocked at how easy that money was to make he said, 'I think I need to have a lie down after making that much money so easily.'

Or take Ava. Back when she was losing money she was using the usual technical analysis methods, but with a full-time job it was pretty much impossible to actually be there when the setups formed, and even then, she'd grab at small profits, take large losses, again all down to emotion as she emptied account after account. I then handed her a set of mechanical rules and pretty much instantly she was using them to bank multiple winning trades, one after the other, bringing in hundreds of dollars with zero thought or stress or emotion, just by following them."

At this stage in the ad, I address the elephant in the room: scepticism. Does this really work? Is this real? Never forget that telling people something raises resistance. However, providing information and letting people draw their own conclusions and tell themselves something works almost always, it results in them believing whatever it is that you're conveying.

For example if you say to your son, "Steve, go and clean your room right now," he'll probably get angry and say no, resisting. On the other hand, saying, "Steve, do you remember that Dad said if you clean your room, he'd take you out for ice cream this evening?" has a different effect. This lets him draw his own conclusion and decide, off his own back, to clean his room, thus removing resistance.

In my ad, I use testimonials that speak for themselves, instead of directly making statements. I usually stick with this formula; [first name] used to [do all the things you're currently doing that aren't working]. Then, they joined me as a client, I gave them [solution] and they got [the result your prospects desire].

"Seriously, if you're losing money as a trader, all you're missing are the rules I'm about to hand you on the next page, so hit the button either top-right if you're on mobile or bottom-left if you're on desktop and believe me, with the rules in hand you'll no longer need to rely on best-guesses, 'technical analysis', indicators, none of it... You'll finally be trading with clarity and with ease, too.

Anyway, I'll see you on the next page, and let's get you results within your trading."

You can watch the ad by visiting:

www.howtotenmillion.com/resources

You now have the necessary knowledge to put out either solid posts, or to write great ads, to garner the attention of prospects who are highly likely to be interested in your offer, and who will soon be flooding into your sales process. Next, let's dive deeper into where to send this traffic, and how to convert the attention into clients, and into dollars.

Qualify, warm up, add value, then sell

It's important to not just create intrigue when attracting prospects by using "wow, not how" style content, or paid ads, but also to add value for them as they enter and move through your sales process. Why is this? Because not all buyers are ready to purchase immediately. Let me share an illustration to better convey this point.

Usually, only three per cent of people are ready to buy on the spot. These are the people who will see an ad, click it, consume your sales material and buy immediately. They are in "buying now" mode. The next tranche of people in "open to it" mode are almost there, but will need a well-written sales page to

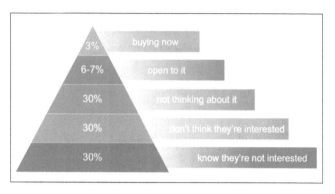

The buyer triangle

read, a call with a sales rep, or perhaps some case studies or testimonials before they buy from you. The next tranche of people in "not thinking about it" mode are similar to those in "open to it" mode, but what you're selling isn't on their mind right now. However, showing them a solid, convincing piece of content or an ad will move them upwards into the "open to it" tranche, which is really the point of our content or ads in the first place.

Prospects in "don't think they're interested" mode, meanwhile, will need more than just content, ads or sales material in order to move up and into the "open to it" and "buying now" tranches. These are the people who will read a sales page, watch a sales video and even have a call with you or your sales team and will still present you with the dreaded, "I'll think about it," objection, even if your offer is what they want and need. The good news is, these people – through the use of email follow-up, retargeting ads, case studies, testimonials, additional content and so on – will eventually rise up into the "open to it" and then the "buying now" tranches given time.

The people in "know they're not interested" mode? They may not be interested now, but, similar to those in "don't think they're interested" mode, can, and often do, become interested given time. In my e-learning company, my sales team would often speak with people on the phone who would say, "I saw your ad and it piqued my interest. My trading is going well, but I'm always interested in new techniques." In other words, they are window shoppers.

Have you ever walked into a shop knowing full well you will not be buying anything, just to pass time? People in "know they're not interested mode" are doing exactly that. So how do we deal with these people? Treat them with the exact same care and respect as anyone else, and again, given time, these people – through the use of email follow-up, retargeting ads, case studies, testimonials, additional content and so on – will eventually rise up into the "open to it" and then the "buying now" tranches.

Action points

This has hopefully given you a really good foundation from which to start scaling and growing your audience. We're going to move on to discuss sales processes next, but before you dive in, go back over this chapter and see if you can write a script for a YouTube ad using the framework I gave you.

Remember to think carefully about what your prospective clients want *and* what they hate/dislike. How can you work that into your ad copy? Follow the formula I set out here and see what you can come up with.

Chapter 5

Sales Processes

Now that you have a good understanding of how to market your information product and attract prospects, it's time to focus on developing your product and the sales process itself. The sales process is most crucial for those who are not ready to buy immediately, and who, therefore, need additional touchpoints with you to reach the "buying now" stage.

Through this sales process, you can tell them who you are, what you do and how you can help them, all while pointing them towards directly making a purchase. Of course, you also need a solid product, even if you're working via a sell-to-build approach, so before we get into the details around sales processes, we'll take a look at the different types of products we can offer as part of an online education business.

This all starts with a product structure, and what you can actually sell to people.

The most common product structures are:

- A front-end course
- An up- or down-sell
- A lead magnet
- A mastermind
- A recurring software or recurring restructured front-end course subscription

Front-end online course

This is simply a collection of videos, laid out in a structure that takes a person from wanting an outcome (that you promise to deliver for them), to having that outcome. These outcomes can be as varied as stopping drinking alcohol, learning to trade, or getting a six pack and so on. It's your call how in-depth or to-the-point you make your course. You have to decide if you offer it with or without a group and with or without coaching or some other form of support, and you also have to decide the price point. You're in control of all of this, but I have a few suggestions to help you along.

Dropping knowledge: pricing your course

I recommend you price the course at what is called a "high-ticket" price. This means at least $2,000 to $3,000. The main reason for this price point is to make your sales income more sustainable if you plan on running ads to your course. Ads can be expensive, so in order to make the numbers work, your price matters. A higher price will also mean higher-quality customers, less complaining and whining, less support, and overall a higher income.

The only reason to sell a course any cheaper is if you either don't believe it's worth paying for, which should indicate that you need to work on the product further to increase its value, or if the "front-end" purchase – which means the first thing a customer will buy – will be followed by an up-sell into a "back-end" product.

A back-end product is anything you sell to existing customers only, such as a high-ticket course, a mastermind or a live-event, or a software. For example, you might sell a $1,000 online course as your "front-end" offer, then a "back-end" $36,000 mastermind for those who want to meet you in-person or become part of a bigger, more valuable group of people who are on the same mission. I've seen that work wonders. Or you might sell a $5,000 online course as your "front-end" offer, then a "back-end" software for $350 per-month that provides help with automations, operations or additional help of some kind in software form.

I'd also strongly suggest adding either one-to-one coaching or group coaching, or both, into your offering. Within my trading education company we do both, and this allows us to charge a slightly higher price on the front-end which, when I sold my company, was $8,500.

When I left, our product structure was as follows: a front-end $8,500 online course with complimentary one-to-one and group-coaching, followed by a $7,000 online mastermind as a primary up-sell, and a $350 per month software as a secondary up-sell. On average, around six per cent of people who bought the front-end would buy the back-end mastermind, and 17 per cent of people would buy the back-end software.

These valuable extras are there for two reasons:

1. To add as much value as possible so that our customers get amazing results.
2. To maximise what's called LTV, or "lifetime value". This is the average total amount of money a customer spends with you across their lifetime.

For example:

- 100 people buy our online course at $9,000 each = $900,000 in sales
- 6 of them also buy our mastermind at $7,000 each = $42,000 in sales
- 17 of them also buy the software at $350 per month = $5,950 in sales

That adds up to $947,950 in sales.

Not bad for only 100 customers!

Up- or down-sells

An up-sell is an extra that you offer your customers, like a mastermind. A down-sell is an extra that you offer to people who decide not to buy your primary offering, like a shorter, smaller version of your online course for perhaps a quarter of the cost.

These are great ways of adding additional revenue to your business, or increasing revenue by bolting it on to a front-end course, like we do with our mastermind. These extras can be anything from monthly one-to-one coaching sessions sold at $100 each, or monthly additional group coaching calls sold for $200 per month, to a "trial" of your course, or a subscription of some kind like an app or a software.

As an example of a down-sell, we offer an alternative version of our front-end program to leads who have not bought, but who have sat on our email list for six months or longer. Instead of the "full" program which includes everything, we down-sell the leads into a version of the program with time-locks that ensures the content unlocks across 12 months, and we charge $350 per month for this "lite" version of the program. This has worked well for us and generates an extra $15,000, or so, per month. That's not a huge amount, but it's recurring and without it, we'd be down by $180,000 per year. It's also entirely cash, which helps towards costs.

A mastermind

This is where most money is made for many online education providers as, similar to the down-sell I just mentioned which is entirely cash, it's usually full-cash-collected and comes with zero acquisition costs, because you're selling it to either an organic audience, or to existing customers who you've already paid to acquire. It can also be the most fun. You get to meet your customers, hang out in person, add massive value via live presentations and bring in guest speakers and teachers.

Regarding what you'll charge, I can give you some guidelines. For one-off events between $8,000 and $14,000 is fair, and for a whole year between $32,000 and $54,000 is fair, depending on your niche and your mastermind offering. For example, you'll charge differently if it's a week on a 100-foot yacht in the Maldives and you're flying your guests in privately, versus if it's a simple weekend at your apartment or house.

You get the picture. The golden rule is to price based on current and future value.

Lead magnets

We all know what these are – an ebook or an audio book, a free-trial of your product or software, a one-off consulting call, a cheat sheet, a free guide in PDF form, etc.

Many people give these away for free, usually in exchange for an email address and/or phone number. However, one tip I'll give you is to charge for these. This will mean you are acquiring buyer leads and filling your email list with people who are invested in what you do, and who've proven that by voting with their wallet and buying your lead magnet. This is a very powerful strategy, because if they've bought one thing, they're much more likely to buy something else; whereas freebie-seekers who'll only get your lead magnet if it's free are, conversely, less likely to buy something.

Recurring software, or restructured front-end

These are by far the most effective products, after a mastermind. A recurring software will add heaps of monthly cash, and it's also cash that will sustain itself if the software is good. This means it'll add reliability and predictability to your company and income.

You could offer some kind of software, or even access to an app, for a monthly fee. Alternatively, you could do what we've done and simply take your front-end course, put time locks on it, replace the high-ticket price with a more affordable monthly price tag, and push this out to your older leads. Ideally these leads will be far outside of your sales cycle, which means it's highly unlikely they would have bought your main program anytime soon.

So, go ahead and take your pick. In an ideal world, you'll align two or three of those to create front-end revenue via, let's say, an online course, and then back-end revenue via a mastermind. If you structure the above properly, you have a six-to-seven-figure company on your hands immediately.

Sales processes

Now we can explore how, specifically, you will sell these products and services – in other words, your sales processes. These are how you take someone from seeing a piece of content or an ad, through to making a purchase from you. I find it helps to think of a sales process as a funnel.

At the top of the funnel, you "pour in" your "traffic" which just means people. You do this by sharing content or running ads. People then see this content and they "enter" your funnel. The bottom of the funnel is where people buy from you. But what happens in the middle of the funnel? I'll share this with you next. Let's dive into exactly how to build, or architect, your sales process funnel.

Funnel structure

The four most common, and effective, types of sales funnel are:

"Free plus shipping" book funnel

This features a book you've written and gives it away "for free" – the buyer simply covers shipping and handling. I highlight the term "for free" because the buyer is actually paying with their contact details and their time and attention in consuming the book itself. Many say this is the most powerful funnel type because it builds huge authority for you as the author, and it creates a huge amount of trust and respect if your book is good.

The reader will fall in love with you, what you do and how you can help them, and this puts them at the top of the buyer triangle in the "buying now" tranche. With their information, you can call them, text them or email them with offers to later convert them into a buyer of your course, coaching program or mastermind.

The funnel is structured as a written sales page with information on the book and how it will help them, alongside a button to buy, which will load a pop-up to collect their name, email and number before sending them to the order form. In many cases, you'll also feature an up-sell on the order form, offering your product, or something similar, at a one-time-only discount. For example, you might offer a "lite" version of your high-ticket course for $497 if they buy it there and then, also adding it to their cart along with your book.

Pricing: Free, but the customer pays for shipping.

"Lead magnet" funnel

This typically gives away an ebook or a free guide in PDF form, or similar. "Isn't this a book?" I hear you ask. It's similar to a standard book, but ebooks and free guides are usually produced with much less in-depth content, whilst being shorter in length, too. Alternatively this might be a cheat sheet, or even a smaller, shorter online course. Again, whatever lead magnet you choose, you'll give it away in return for a person's contact details and their time and attention in consuming the item you provide them.

The funnel is structured in the same way as the previous example, where you have a written sales page (sharing similar information), a button to buy, a data capture form and an up-sell if they add it to their cart along with your lead magnet.

Pricing: Usually free, but charging a small fee of around $7 for an ebook, or perhaps $47 for a "lite" version of a course can work well for building a list of buyer leads.

"Book a call" funnel

This type of funnel provides value within the sales presentation, also known as a VSL which stands for value sales letter. This is a short five to 15-minute video that explains who you are and how you can help, along with outlining the problem you're able to solve, or the knowledge you're able to share with the prospect. Its purpose is to firstly provide value. But its secondary purpose is to entice the prospect by highlighting their problem and sharing how you're able to solve it for them. The final step in this type of funnel is a call to action, which in this case is booking a "strategy session" call with you or a member of your team.

The funnel is structured with the opt-in page that reaffirms the promise or offer along with collecting the person's name, email and phone number. When they click submit, they'll go to a VSL page, followed by a calendar page if they choose to book a call. Once a call is booked, they're sent to a "thank you for booking" page where you'll share client testimonials, results, proof or anything of that nature to reaffirm that they've made a great decision by booking a call.

Pricing: $3,000 minimum, right up to $10,000+ depending on the offer.

"Webinar" funnel

This type of funnel provides value within the sales presentation, which in this case is a long-form webinar, typically running for between 45 minutes on the shorter side, and two-plus hours on the longer side. The webinar is similar to a VSL, but much slower and much more in-depth. It will explain who you are, how you can help, your story and how you went from "zero to hero" as you learned and mastered what you'll be helping the prospect to achieve, and more. At the end of the webinar, you will either sell the offer there and then or, as I prefer to do, you will ask them to book a call to discuss purchasing.

The funnel is structured in a very similar way to the "book a call" funnel, with an opt-in page that reaffirms the promise or offer and collects the person's contact details, but the difference is, the prospect will now select a day and a time to attend the webinar. When they click submit, they'll go to a confirmation page and if set up this way, they can even watch the webinar there and then. This is called an "on demand" webinar. These typically convert prospects into customers at a lower rate than a live webinar because there's no human connection as it's pre-recorded or is a recording from a past webinar, but they are more scalable as they aren't tied to your human time like a live webinar is.

Pricing; From $997 to no more than $1,997 if you're selling whilst on the webinar. Any more and it's very difficult to get prospects to pay there and then as, usually, larger amounts require a one-to-one consultation before a purchase decision can be made. This is why book-a-call funnels are usually only for high-ticket products and services, because they are ideal for building a stronger human connection, whereas webinar *funnels are better for entry-level products that require less of that relationship building to sell.*

Action points

You can go ahead and take your pick of the products and sales funnels I've outlined in this chapter. When you choose a product and sales funnel structure, you are one step closer to building your online education business.

Do you already have some thoughts about which product would suit you best? Did any of the sales funnel structures I shared stand out to you? If so, write them down. You might not know exactly how it's all going to work yet, but now you have an outline of a plan.

Of course, you now need to write a sales page or sales video script, and if calls are part of your sales process then you'll need a process and script for conducting those too. This is precisely what we're going to cover next, and I'll even share the word-for-word script that the sales team in my e-learning company uses to close prospects like clockwork.

AudioBook

Do you like listening as much as reading?

Listen to My Personally Recorded Audiobook

Get your **FREE** *Audiobook now!*
SCAN THE QR CODE

Chapter 6

The Illusion of Sales

Sales truly are the be-all and end-all of a business.

I can't overstate this – sales are the most crucial aspect of success, and as a business owner, it's your most important responsibility. Your business' success does not rest on the quality of your product or service, or that of your team or even your marketing. They can all fail and still, if you are able to generate sales and thus put capital in the bank, you can fix those aspects and dominate the market, making yourself extremely rich in the process. If, on the other hand, you cannot generate sales, you can have the world's best product, team, marketing, everything, and it's all for nothing.

If sales intimidates you, however, don't worry – you're not alone as many people feel this way.

There are two types of salespeople...

The first is an old-school, classic slimy, pushy, aggressive a**hole who thinks they are above others, and who rams offers down people's throats whether they're good for them or not, all for the largest pay-cheque they can get.

The second is someone like me and you, who understands that a sales call is nothing but a helpful, valuable call where we help our prospects reach the best decision for them, whether that is a "yes" or a "no". We use the call to educate them, add value for them, show them we're able to help them, answer their questions and address any queries or concerns. From there, they either join and we help them achieve their desired result, or they do not join and we wish them the best.

The Illusion of Sales

Sales has a negative connotation, but it needn't.

What I just described above is how easy, and how great, sales calls are. Heck, at my e-learning company we don't even call them sales calls. We call them decision-based coaching calls, because that's what they truly are. If we really boil it down, your job on a sales call is to have a polite, respectful, value-led conversation.

Better yet, we are not forcing anyone to book in with us. Our prospects are wilfully choosing to book these calls to discuss our offer and our services, after being intrigued by our sales process. How is it "selling" when people are coming to us asking for help and info on what we offer? It isn't.

That is the illusion of sales. For us, it doesn't even exist. We don't sell, we educate. We don't sell, we add value. We don't sell, we have a polite, respectful conversation. We don't sell, we ask questions that enable the prospect to understand how we can help, so that they can reach their own decision – yes or no. What I'm about to share with you is the most integrity-led, value-led and prospect-focused way to "sell", ensuring that we show respect and are respected, so that we all win – our prospects willingly and easily buy, and we happily and enjoyably serve them at the highest level.

How to write a sales page that sells anything, to anyone, with ease

The main thing to remember when you're writing or creating sales material is that you're simply helping people make the right decision for them. For an online education business, you'll need a written sales page. Luckily for you, I have created a very simple formula that makes the process easy.

In fact, if you've ever visited and read through the "Join My Community" page of the website behind the e-learning company that I used to own, then you've seen the formula in action. It's as simple as the following steps:

- If you're on this page, I'm going to presume that you're here because... [insert problem].
- You're tired of... [problem, thing they're unsure of, thing they're worried about].
- If that's the case, I can help... [explain how].
- If I could share... [helpful and valuable info].
- How would that impact your... [problem].

Can you see what we're doing here? Right from the off we're calling out who should, and who should not, be reading the page. We're calling out their pains, problems and worries. Straight away, we're telling them that we can help, along with briefly telling them how. Let's continue:

- To tell you exactly how my [insert solution] works... [explain how it works].
- I know what you're thinking, is this real... [address their scepticism].
- In fact, check this out, below... [insert graphic proof of results].
- But, don't take my word for it... [insert testimonials].

Here, we've established some ground regarding "how what we do works" but we've kept it "wow, not how" based. We've also addressed any early scepticism and we've provided physical examples of both cold, hard proof in addition to testimonials. Let's keep going...

- Sound too good to be true? My client [insert client name from above] thought that too... [insert specific client result]. Imagine achieving [solution] for yourself. And the best part? All [client] did to achieve that was [insert push-button style explanation, using the "what they want, without what they hate" technique].
- It took me weeks and months to [insert a brief part of your journey mastering what you're teaching] but it was all worth it. I used to make all of the usual mistakes... [insert the two or three most common mistakes your prospects face].
- The thing is, without [solution] you're toast. You'll struggle to succeed without it, and yet it's exactly what [your unique offer] provides. And if you're thinking "why haven't I heard of [your unique solution] before" [insert

simple explanation as to why]. Then again, most people struggle with [main pain point] so why are you currently doing what they do?

- When I learned about [solution] I escaped the pain of [main pain point people experience] and there's absolutely nothing stopping you from doing the same. Listen, can I just share [solution] with you?

- Imagine you [learned solution] and you [got your promised outcome]. Picture yourself, right now, not having to [suffer with main pain point]. Imagine removing [second pain point]. How would that impact your [insert industry you sell to i.e. trading/fitness etc]?

In this section, we are zeroing in on proof, sharing more of our story, and we're slowly triggering their imagination in regards to what's to come when they've bought our offer, solved their pain and are getting their desired result. We are using powerful thought-provoking words like "imagine", and we're asking them, "How would that impact your...?" in order to future-pace what we'll soon be helping them to achieve.

- Would you like to [get solution] along with my personal help? If so, I've built a [insert a tiny bit of info on your offer, product or service]. By the end of it, you're ready to [get result]. But what you're really getting isn't just [minor desired outcome], you're getting control, you're gaining confidence and you're finally going to gain [major desired outcome].
- All you need to do is [insert "what they want, without the things they hate" style description]. And no, the [offer, product or service] is not confusing or overly detailed. It's [insert a simple, push-button style description]. If [client name] can do it, why can't you? [insert testimonial]. And if [client name] can do it, why can't you? [insert testimonial]. And if [client name] can do it, why can't you? [insert testimonial].
- Your job is simple. Learn [solution], apply [what they'll learn] and get [desired outcome]. So what are you waiting for? Join now... [insert buy button, book a call button or a graphic showing everything they'll get, then a buy button below it].

Here, for the first time on the page, we give the reader a call to action. This comes after we've politely offered them info on our solution, and also gone as far as to ask them, "Would you like my personal help?" At this stage of the sales page, those people at the bottom of the buyer triangle will click off and leave, and those buyers at the top of the buyer triangle will make a purchase.

But what about the people in the other parts of the buyer triangle? They'll take a little more convincing and will require a little more information, detail and explanation. So, to help with this, we include the following:

- As soon as you've joined the program, you will have instant access to [insert what they'll get access to]. From there, you will be able to [attend coaching sessions, get extras, join our private group]. You'll also receive [anything else they get].
- And as if all of that value isn't enough, see our guarantee [insert refund guarantee]. We offer a 100 per cent money-back guarantee making your purchase entirely risk-free. Simply put, our [product] either provides [desired outcome] or you get your money back. All we ask is that you [insert your terms, or what they have to do to qualify]. Your success and results truly are the priority. So what are you waiting for? Let's get you started [insert call to action].
- But I can't share [offer, product or service] forever. I pride myself on providing the absolute best service to my clients, and I can only do that for a limited number of people at a time. That's why I only let [number] of new

clients in per month, so that I can uphold such a high standard of service.

- I make that promise to you, just like I've made it to my other clients, so for the above reasons, I will be removing [offer, product or service] from sale when my community reaches a certain size. So don't wait to join me in [getting result].

- But if you'd prefer to carry on [struggling with pain] I can't stop you. If you'd prefer to carry on [insert two or three struggles or pain points], again, I can't stop you doing that. What I can do however is help you to [get result] without [what they hate]. If you'd prefer the second option, then [insert call to action].

By this stage of the page, in most cases, the people who were in the "open to it" tranche of the buyer triangle will have purchased or booked a call and, at the very least, the people in the "not thinking about it" and "don't think they're open to it" tranches will have moved up slightly, too. And if not? No problem. We will continue to deliver value to them via retargeting ads, additional content or specific emails that we'll send to them in a day or two, and keep nudging them up the buyer triangle until they reach the top.

And that's a wrap. Take the above framework, combine it with the tips, techniques and strategies I've shared with you thus far, write out your own sales page, and you're all set! If you follow my advice, you'll have a solid, finished sales page that's ready to go.

As a helping hand, I'm providing an exact clone of our sales page – the one that's made us over $2,000,000 – for you to download and clone straight into your ClickFunnels classic account.

Download an exact clone of our sales page, here:

www.howtotenmillion.com/resources

How to write a webinar or a VSL that makes you $1,000,000

You now know how to write a sales page that will almost certainly convert at a high level. For those of you who have the time and budget, hiring a copywriter to either do the above for you, or double-check your work before going live, will ensure that the copy is spot on. A professional opinion goes a long way – that's why I offer one-to-one coaching for business owners, to make absolutely sure that they are doing everything right, to save time and costly mistakes.

Next, let me share with you how to write a webinar or a VSL that makes you $1,000,000. I'll do this by sharing an example of one that I wrote for one of my business coaching clients, Nathan, which has – as of me writing this book – brought in over $200,000 in total sales volume for him and his business.

Would you be happy earning that amount from your online education business?

How to produce a VSL

Before we journey into writing a value sales letter, let me now share another concept with you: New, Easy, Safe, Big. Also known as the "NESB" concept, it was invented by world-famous copywriter, Kyle Milligan. For those who don't know of Kyle, he is a professional copywriter who has made multiple millions of dollars writing high-converting emails and sales letters across his career.

Simply put, Kyle is one of the best in the world at writing words that convert readers into buyers. I'd also strongly encourage you to read his book, *Take Their Money.* It's one of the simplest yet best copywriting books ever written, and it's where I myself learned of the "NESB" formula – what I'd like you to understand is that writing words that turn readers into buyers is simple, if you follow the right formula. "NESB" makes this easier, much easier.[2]

"New" means making sure that your offer, product or service is positioned as something new and unique – in other words, something you created or invented, or a new twist or take on something that exists.

"Easy" means making sure that you're standing by the push-button way of conveying the value in your offer, product or

---

2   Milligan K., (2022), *Take Their Money: How To Write The Words That Really Make You Rich,* Amazon Kindle

service. There's a good example of this in my ad copy, where I used the "what they want, without anything they hate" framework.

"Safe" means making sure that prospects believe that what you're offering is achievable, and that it will work for them. After all, if your offer, product or service is positioned as extremely complex, difficult and time-consuming, I'm sorry to say this, but it's simply not what the majority of humans want to buy. Humans want things that are new, easy, safe and, finally, "big".

This final part of the formula, "big", means making sure that your offer, product or service is positioned as being a "big" deal, or a "big" opportunity. It needs to be positioned as a breakthrough, or something that's exciting!

Don't worry, you don't have to use every aspect of the "NESB" formula. If you're struggling, or you think that one or two don't apply, that's OK. One or two is great, two or three is fantastic, and if you can use all four? That is ideal, and you're likely going to do extremely well and make a lot of money.

Take care of the logistics too

Now that we've covered the "NESB" formula, let's cover some more logistical aspects of writing and building a VSL before I share the script. The logistical and practical elements of a VSL are just as important as your script, and it pays to take some time to plan for them.

For example, if you're shooting an in-person VSL, make sure you align your clothing, hair style and environment with your target client. As an example, if you "sell the dream lifestyle" to younger people, then you should be well-dressed, wear a nice watch, film with a T-shirt or polo shirt on, in a nice office or a lounge with a professional setup. If you sell a consulting service, then wear a blazer and shoes, in a nice office with perhaps a city view behind you à la Sam Ovens, whilst wearing a nice watch, styling your hair and so on.

Or, if you sell let's say professional services to men aged 35 and older, then you should wear a shirt and be in a nice office with a professional setup. Alternatively, let's say you sell baby products to women, in which case you should dress like a mum, perhaps film in your lounge with a solid well-dressed background in a house setting that shows you've done well for yourself, but with no fancy watch or affluent items. Be down to earth, as your target client would be themselves.

Whatever your target audience, think "tribe", because, typically, humans want to spend time with, dress like, and act like people who are like them. Similarly, think "stereotype", because these exist for a reason.

Birds of a feather flock together.

Top tactics for creating a successful VSL

First on the list is a point I've already made in relation to sales copy, but it's so important it bears repeating. Never make what you're selling out to be difficult. If there is any difficulty involved, use language like "I've found a secret way to do…" or "here's a new way to…" The key is pointing out that your way doesn't involve hard work, is fast or is easy with little to no risk. I know you might think this comes across as "spammy", but it's human nature that we won't proceed if we get even the slightest hint of hard work.

With that said, I want to add a caveat here regarding what I call 'market polarity'. This is something I learned through my career as a professional trader, whereby 'A' can, when overdone, transform into 'B'.

As an example, if everyone in your niche or market is saying 'zig' then I strongly advise you to 'zag', if it is doable and is appropriate. For example, when I began my e-learning company in the trading space, almost every single educational offer on the market was centred around technical analysis, a type of trading involving discretionary choices made based on analysing financial markets manually. This was the 'zig' most offers were built around. I realised this, and chose to 'zag' instead, by saying that I'd discovered a new way of trading without analysis, without discretion and without emotion, by using 'mechanical trading rules'. This allowed me to instantly stand out in the market and it gave me an extremely strong edge. I zagged where everyone else zigged, creating extreme market polarity.

Sometimes, going against the grain can give you a strong and instantaneous edge and will help you to stand out in your niche and market. So, where appropriate, think about how you can challenge the status quo and 'zag' when everyone else is trying to 'zig'.

Secondly, revisit the rest of the "NESB" concept once you've got the "easy" part covered. If your prospects have the remotest idea that they might have tried what you are offering before, they will not buy. If they consider for a second that it might be risky or unsafe, they will leave and go back to whatever they were looking at elsewhere. The "new" and "safe" parts of the formula are the important ones to look at, alongside the ease of your solution.

Thirdly, use stories to remove people's potential objections. The aim is to preempt the most likely objections you expect from your audience and allay these fears by showing that what you're sharing worked for someone else.

Fourthly, use pattern interrupts where possible, but without overusing them. Throwing in the odd swear word, an unusual analogy or something funny will help keep the viewer's attention. For example, in my VSL, at one stage I say something like "Now, let's just cut the shit, because..." with a picture of scissors and an emoji poo. This causes the viewer to snap back into the present moment if they are becoming disengaged, or doing something else whilst watching.

Tip five is to focus on your tone. By that I mean make sure you don't sound commercial or like a television news presenter. Speak as if you're talking to a friend when you meet up with them for coffee – you're aiming for natural and confident. Also, make sure you vary your pitch and speed. Refer to my VSL for a good example of this, as one of my strongest natural skills is variance in tonality, speed and cadence.

Number six is to keep your VSL short and make sure you're only covering what you absolutely need to. Remember that people have short attention spans. Use techniques like tonality, pattern interrupts and high-quality slides with great design elements to keep viewers focused. If your VSL ends up on the longer side, here's a hack for you – when your video is done, put it in a video editor and speed it up by 0.1x to shave a few minutes off the length. Just make sure it doesn't affect your vocal tone.

Tip seven is extremely important – always remember that none of this is about you, it's about the viewer, their wants and needs, and the pain they are here to solve. Don't ever talk at length about yourself, your product or your story. Definitely don't mention pricing, discounts or anything that is sales'y or you will instantly break trust. Remember, the purpose of a VSL is to convey the value that your offer, product or solution provides.

Number eight is to use "loops" and not close them. This will keep people watching. For example, tell them you'll map out the steps to do X, Y or Z, but don't give them the steps at that point. Instead talk about something else relating to their pain or problem. In many cases, the viewer will be left thinking, "When will this person tell me the steps? Tell me the steps!" and they have entered your loop, which you will not close, thus keeping them watching.

Finally, you need to "widen the gap" between where the viewer is now, and where they want to get to, because if people believe they can solve their problem or remove their pain without you, they will not buy. By widening the gap, you become the bridge they need to finally achieve their dream outcome and they will buy from you.

To see how this all works in practice, you can watch the last VSL I personally wrote and produced for my e-learning company before I exited, which made well over $7,500,000.

Download it here: www.howtotenmillion.com/resources

The ideal VSL script

Before I walk you through the script I wrote for my business coaching client Nathan so that you can see inside a multi six-figure VSL, I want to share with you the core building blocks that most often stand behind high-performing VSL scripts.

You do not need to use all of these, nor do you need to order them as I have below. These are simply the core pillars. You'll use those that are appropriate to your offer, based on your niche and market, along with the type of avatar that you're selling to, where they are on the 'buyer triangle', their level of scepticism, and so on.

Call out the ideal viewer: Here, call out your ideal avatar. Be as detailed as possible. For example, you might say: "If you are someone who is [ideal avatar, describe them] then keep watching, because..."

Big promise, with a time limitation: Here, make them a big promise while also telling them how long it will take you to explain everything, ideally in a short amount of time. For example, you might say: "In the next [amount of minutes], I'm going to [share with you, or show you, or reveal to you] how you can [get outcome, or learn to achieve result, or achieve desired outcome]."

Establish authority: Here, you'll establish your authority by saying something like: "My name is [your name], and I [big, bold claim about yourself to position you as an authority, or stamp your credibility, or assert your authority or paint you as someone who should be listened to]."

Big claim and why you: Here, make a big claim and explain why you're able to deliver on it. For example, you might say: "I'm able to [do, or achieve]" and then "[big claim, or big promise]" and then "because I [know, or have been, or have done, or have experienced]" and then "[x, z, y]."

Open a loop to keep them watching: Here, you'll open a loop in order to entice the viewer to keep watching. For example, you might say: "And to map out the key steps I've walked through to [achieve what I've achieved, or get to where I am today, or attain the dream outcome I've been able to attain], well, let me just get straight to the point because I know that your time is valuable..."

Authority figures to back up your claim/s: Here, you'll share some authority figures to cement your claim/s, if appropriate. For example, you might say: "And it's not just me, either. X person of [fame] has been doing this... Y person of [credibility] has been doing this... Z person of [authority] has been doing this..."

Urgency: Here, you'll create urgency. For example, you might say: "But this window of opportunity won't last forever, and the doors are quickly closing. This is a brand new discovery, and others will pile on it as they discover this for themselves in the coming weeks and months. You must act now."

Proof: Here, you'll prove to them it has worked for you, for others, and that it can work for them, too. Share hard-proof such as bank statements, press articles, testimonials, video footage, screenshots of WhatsApp messages or Instagram messages or similar.

Third-party credibility: Here, you'll share third-party credibility with them. For example, you might say: "There's a reason that I [or your system, or your company, or your offer] have been featured in [insert press articles, key videos, high-profile podcasts, interviews or websites]."

Pre-empt objections and know-it-alls: Here, you'll pre-empt and remove the key objections that your viewers are likely to hold in mind. For example, you might say: "And no, it has nothing to do with [what they expect it to be about, or are concerned that it may involve], plus this can be done without [objection], without [objection] and without ever [objection], either."

Let them in on a secret only the elite know of: Here, you'll show them how the elite figures in your specific niche or market have been doing it for themselves, or how it's worked for them or benefited them. Think athletes, millionaires, billionaires, executives, famous professionals, celebrities and so on.

Share your story of discovery: Here, you'll explain how you stumbled on your niche, market or solution. Remember, facts tell, but stories sell. When someone listens to a story, they see themselves as the protagonist, so it's useful to tell your story in a way that aligns with your prospects current situation and ideal situation if possible.

Widen the gap: Here, you'll widen the gap between where they are now, and where they want to get to. For example, you might say: "Imagine this for a second... Imagine [paint the picture of where they want to get to]. Lay your scepticism aside for a second, and just imagine what that would feel like..."

Restate the big promise: Here, you'll restate the main, big promise you're making to the prospect. For example, you might say: "That's why I've been able to [big claim] and why you can do it, too."

Present the scarce opportunity: Here, you'll present the scarce opportunity. For example, you might say: "But this won't last forever, because..." and then justify the reason why they must act now.

Share proof that it works: Here, you'll share proof for a second time that it works, to increase how complicit the viewers are, and in turn, how receptive they'll likely be when you make your first call-to-action. For example, you might say: "Like I said earlier, this is by far the best, and is certainly the fastest way to [get outcome, or achieve desire, or solve problem] that's out there today, because..."

The altruistic reason why: Here, you'll give a reason which can be almost anything, as to why you're making this video and helping people with what you're helping them with. When humans hear the word 'because' it causes the brain to automatically begin reducing scepticism. For example, you might say: "And if you're wondering why I'm doing this, it's only because I've [gotten everything I ever wanted, or have made more money than I'll ever need] and, therefore, I'm in a position to [give back, or help other people who are still stuck where I was]."

Future pace: Here, you'll future-pace the prospects' desires, causing them to focus on what they'll achieve by working with you, or investing in your product or service. For example, you might say: "Here's what will happen when you start using [offer]..."

Pattern interrupt: Here, you'll add in an abrupt pattern interrupt that stands out and, if they've begun to drift off, pulls them back into the present moment and makes them pay full attention once again. For example, you might say: "But stop, because I can hear your bullshit detector ringing louder than the scream of an African banshee...". It can help to add in just one or two swear words throughout a VSL, if appropriate to your niche and market, because swear words trigger emotional arousal in the brain and increase attention.

Additional proof: Here, you'll share more proof to further cement that this is easy, safe and anybody can do it. Share unarguable types of proof such as bank statements, press articles, testimonials, video footage, screenshots of WhatsApp messages or Instagram messages or similar.

Transition to the pitch for the call and give a call-to-action: Here, you'll transition to your pitch for the sales call you want them to book, before giving them a call-to-action. For example, you might say: "I've created [offer, or product, or program] that will help you to [get outcome, or achieve desires] just like I have, and I call it [the name of your product, program or business]. By booking a call below, I'll be able to [explain what will happen on the call]."

Risk-reversal: Here, you'll insert your money-back guarantee if necessary in the context of your offer, or justify the reason for the call. One reason I've found to work well is explaining that it is not a "sales call" and whilst you will share more info on how you can help them through your product or service, it will be a valuable call for them whether they buy or not.

Call to action: Here, you'll insert your second and final call-to-action. For example, you might say: "Just below this video, you'll see a button that says [what it says on your button i.e. 'book your free strategy session now' or 'check call booking availability and reserve your slot now' or something similar]," and then "I want you to click that button and book a call with me right now..."

Urgency: Here, you'll add some final urgency before wrapping up. For example, you might say: "Like I said earlier, this window of opportunity won't last forever, and the doors are quickly closing. This is a brand new discovery, and others will pile on it as they, too, discover it for themselves. You must act now."

Final future-pace: Here, you'll share your final future-pace which will align with your ideal prospects' desires, causing them to focus on what they'll achieve by working with you, or investing in your product or service. For example, you might end by saying: "There are better times ahead, and you'll soon be able to [achieve desired outcome, solve problems, remove pain, or similar] just like I have and just like others have, too. This is the start of [a better life, more money, better health, more freedom, or similar]."

There you have it. Those are the most common and most effective building blocks behind high-converting VSL scripts. With those covered, let me share with you the VSL script I wrote for my business coaching client Nathan, which made him over $200,000 in sales as of me writing this book. See if you can spot some of the building blocks from the above list as we move through it.

"Hi, my name's Nathan and I'm the founder of a seven-figure business that just a few years ago allowed me to bid farewell to the soul-destroying rat-race that many of us get stuck in, and the crazy thing is, and you're probably not expecting me to say this, but setting the business up

The Illusion of Sales

and growing it was one of the easiest, simplest and fastest things I've ever done."

We're only a minute or two in here, but we've already added in a future result that our prospects are likely to want – a seven-figure business, along with bidding farewell to the soul-destroying rat race – and we've also used the push-button technique by saying; "It was one of the easiest, simplest and fastest things I've ever done."

> "And to map out the steps I walked through to do that... Well, let me just get straight to the point because I know that your time is valuable... If you're someone who hates their job, who on a Sunday afternoon feels that bone-chilling anxiety of yet another week stuck in a job that you hate, all to make someone else rich. If you're someone who wants to take their family on 'that' holiday that you promised you'd deliver on, but that you still can't afford, or buy themselves 'that' car you've always dreamed of, that you, again, still can't afford. If you're lacking freedom and, let's be honest, you want to make money as fast and as easily as possible, then you might just have found the answer."

Here, we've opened a loop to ensure the viewer gets hooked in and keeps watching, and we've directly called out who should be watching: someone who hates their job, who can't afford life's luxuries, and so on. We've also used the push-button technique yet again by saying, "If you want to make money as fast and as easily as possible, then you might have just found the answer."

"Let me explain what I'm talking about, and to do so, I'll start with my story... See, not too long ago, I was in that position that I've just described. The Sunday anxiety ahead of yet another working-week, the back-stabbing employees and their drama and problems they always wanted to tell me about, the holidays I'd promised my wife, but couldn't deliver on, seeing other people win in life, whilst I was – to put it plainly – a wage-slave, wasting my life making someone else rich.

I started out working in London in 2009 and after a few job changes trying to find something I enjoyed, I began a position at a law firm which, in the end, I wasted 11 long years of my life stuck in, and maybe you can relate. Maybe you're stuck in a job right now that's sucking the life out of you, too.

I wanted out, and if I'm honest with myself, I just wanted two things: money and freedom. Again, maybe you want those same things, too. I wanted to start my own business, be in control of my life and my time, to work when I wanted, go on holiday when I wanted, to treat my family to the things they wanted...

But I didn't have a donkey's clue how to get there. How the hell do I start a business? How do I fund starting a business? What business should I start? What if I fail? What will I do if I fail? Those were the questions I was asking myself as my mind spun in circles on yet another anxiety-filled Sunday afternoon with the dread of another upcoming Monday morning. Until everything changed in an instant."

Here, we're using the story technique that I mentioned in tip number three, to build relatability with the ideal prospect. We're describing the situation that *they* are likely currently in themselves, which builds trust and deepens the "like, know and trust" factor they'll have with Nathan, making them more likely to book a call, and later, to make a purchase. Also, look at how I've included, "Maybe you want those things, too" in order to trigger a response in the prospect's mind, where they say to themselves, *wow, yes, that is what I want. This guy really knows me and my situation.* This all strengthens their relationship with Nathan.

"One morning, as I was stuck in traffic in the pouring rain whilst driving to work, there was a program on the radio that talked about starting a service business. It talked about how fast and easy it was to set one up. How much money could be made, and for the rest of the day, I felt this warm, fuzzy excitement in my stomach. I couldn't stop thinking about how this "might just be the answer" that I was looking for.

I went home that night, I started Google searching "how to start a service business" and I decided, what do I have to lose? I thought to myself, if I don't at least try to do this, try to do my own thing in life, to take a chance, I'll just stay stuck in the same 9-5 loop for years to come.

That thought of staying stuck, staying broke, scared the life out of me, so I went for it. I decided, enough is enough. I have to take action, and the next weekend I spent the whole of Saturday thinking of a name for my upcoming service business, registering a website address, and making a list of people I could cold call to make my first sales, all of that stuff.

What happened? Well, that was four years ago now, and in the end, it ended up taking me five months to make my first sale, because I had no direction, I had no knowledge, I had no money and I thought that making a website, cold calling, all of that rubbish was the way to get clients. I was wrong. Very wrong. I now know that you don't need to do any of that."

Here, we're painting the picture of how Nathan stumbled on his "unique opportunity" and how it came together for him. We're also adding in how it took him "5 months to make his first sale" because he had "no direction, no knowledge" and so on. This is crucial, because we want prospects to understand that it is extremely difficult to do it alone with no help and we're handling their objections. In doing so, we're priming them for the push-button solution Nathan offers.

"You don't need to cold call. You don't need lots of money. You don't need to wait months to make a sale. You don't need some big, shiny brand or logo. You don't even need much time and you definitely don't need any experience to start and grow a service business, you can do it rapidly. In fact I've shared my secret to doing it all in a matter of just days with a couple of friends over the last few months and they've been able to hit five and in one case, even six figures, inside of less than 30 days.

(Yes, I did just say you could make six figures in less than 30 days. And I'll prove it in a second)."

Now we've covered what they want, with none of the things they hate.

"But coming back to my point, using what I've learned, if we fast forward to the present day I now run a very successful service company, I've even had the pleasure of working on a service job for companies like Tesla, Ford and Google, and I consistently, routinely make well over $100,000 per month.

Each day I wake up, I jump out of bed, I plan my day and can't even begin to tell you how much I look forward to the working week. My Sundays are no longer filled with dread, I spend them with my family, doing endless activities, enjoying roast dinners together and I never experience Sunday anxiety like I used to before.

My old life is, well, just that. My old life. And my new life? If I could have dreamed of my perfect life, that's the life I live today. Now, picture this for me because I want you to experience that feeling for yourself...

Imagine the feeling of joy, freedom, never wanting for anything. Waking up every day knowing that with every passing month, five to six figures will hit your bank account, predictably and repeatedly. Imagine checking your bank account and seeing over six-figures sitting there, ready to be invested, ready to buy that dream car or your dream house, ready to book that dream holiday you've always wanted to book.

Be honest with yourself and for just a second, lay aside your scepticism and allow yourself to dream. If all of what I've just said came true for you, how would that make you feel?"

Here, we're "widening the gap" and causing separation between where they are now and where they desire to be in the future, by using words like "imagine". This is one of the most powerful words you can say to a human, as it directly triggers a person's imagination to fire and we're painting a picture of how their life *could* look.

"Now, if you're wondering what the hells bells a service company is, or what it does, or how you might be able to set one up and jump up to the six-figure per-month mark as quickly and easily as I mentioned is possible earlier in the video, that's where I might be able to help. See, I went from stuck in a life I hated. Stressed, lost, looking for a way out. I made every mistake in the book, but in the end, I got there.

And all the mistakes aside, I did one thing right; I documented every step I took. I documented the things I did right, the many things I did wrong by going it alone and trying to figure it all out on my own. And through all of that, I've put together a 3-step process that anyone can follow. In fact, if you're watching this right now and you're thinking "I'd love to achieve what this guy has achieved", the time-freedom, the financial freedom, all of it, then this is for you."

Here, we're introducing the possibility of an offer that the prospect can purchase, and we're using a story to introduce it to provide proof that it works. We've also included the phrase "anyone can follow" to directly capture the ease of the solution for the first time. The prospect is now aware that there may be a way for them to close the gap on their desires by purchasing something, and they know Nathan, his story and achievements, and are likely to want to achieve the same things.

"I call it the 'service industry blueprint' and believe it or not – I promised you I'd deliver, didn't I – I'm going to hand it over free of charge for the first 25 people who book in a strategy session call with me over the next ten days. Because I know that if I can just stop even one person from making all of the mistakes I made, wasting all of the money I wasted, the fulfilment I'll take from that will be worth the small time commitment on my part.

So, just below this video, you should see a 'book a call' button. I want you to click that button right now, book a call with me, and on the call, I'll hand over the blueprint for you and personally walk you through each step that you need to take to start and scale a service business in the next 30 days."

Here, we've finally offered our first call to action and we are being extremely direct in our words because our viewers' attention is finite, so it's crucial that we grab their attention and tell them exactly what to do.

We've also positioned the call as a helpful session with Nathan where you'll be handed his "service industry blueprint" cheat sheet, which takes the weight off of booking the call and removes sales resistance. Nathan hands out the "service industry blueprint" before each call, using an automatic email that fires when someone books a call. This is his lead magnet, written in a "wow, not the how" style, designed to get prospects excited before they speak to him.

"And don't worry, the call is completely free and it is **not** a sales call. So why am I taking up my time doing these calls over the next ten days? It's simple... I know that if I speak with 25 people and hand over all of the value I have to share, one or two of those people might also want my personal help and guidance, which I do charge a fee for, **but** again, if you just want to jump on a call, speak to someone like me who's achieved what you want to achieve and who makes over $100,000 per month, and take my blueprint from me and go it alone, that's no problem at all.

So again, hit the 'book a call' button below this video right now, choose a day and a time with me, let's jump on a call together and I will personally speak to you and map out for you exactly what to do, exactly how to do it, and exactly how you can start and scale a service-business in literally just a matter of days, and scale it up to six-figs per month in income for yourself and your family.

It's really not as hard as some people out there want you to believe. And the minute you have the blueprint that I'll be sharing with you on the call, you'll know that to be true. I'll leave you with this...

If I can do it, anyone can. I hated my life, I hated my job, I lived in stress and fear and anxiety and worry, and I got through it all and I now own a simple business that's easy and fun to run, and that adds over six-figures per month to my bank account.

On our call together, I'll show you exactly how I did it. So that you can do the same. There are better times ahead, so book a call with me right now, and here's to the next chapter of your life. Speak to you soon."

Finally, we've offered a second strong call to action, and we've also mentioned that there will be an opportunity to purchase something whilst on the call, for those who want to work directly with Nathan. We're not here to twist anybody's arm or lie to them. We're here to share value and to let those who want to invest in themselves do so.

Action points

That's how simple it is to write a killer sales page and VSL script. All you need to do is watch my VSL that I linked you to above, read through and reference Nathan's VSL for inspiration, and slowly begin to utilise the techniques I've taught you, and you'll soon have a $1,000,000 VSL for yourself.

You can also work your way through the sales page I shared, tailoring it to suit your offering and industry – why not take some time now to write both your sales page and VSL script? With the outlines I've shared here, these shouldn't take you too long!

Don't Forget William's 16.4M Dollar Resources

Scan the QR Code Below

Chapter 7

Building Your Funnel and Writing Your Pitch

Your VSL is a very important part of your sales funnel, but it isn't the only component. There are four simple steps to the sales call funnel that I'll share with you in this chapter:

1. Opt-in page, which will be used to state your offer and promise in a "wow, not how" fashion and collect the prospects' info i.e. name, email, phone number.
2. VSL page where you'll host your VSL alongside a "book a call" button.
3. Schedule page which will include your calendar and availability.
4. Thank you page, which will have a short video of you thanking them for booking, explaining next steps and

some testimonials, and perhaps some results from yourself, clients, or both.

As a helping-hand, I'm providing an exact clone of our call funnel, the one that's made us over $15,000,000, for you to download and clone straight into your ClickFunnels classic account. You can use this and swap out my elements for your own elements.

Download an exact clone of our $15,000,000 funnel at:

www.howtotenmillion.com/resources

Here are the four steps to a simple sales call funnel, mapped out in detail for you.

Opt-in

On this page, you'll do three things:

1. Write a catchy headline that reaffirms your offer, and conveys the value in the prospect submitting their info in return for being allowed through to watch the "free training" on the following page.
2. Add in two or three bullet-points of text that briefly explain, in a "wow, not how" style, what they can expect from the training.
3. Add an image that brings the page to life. Don't worry, the image is not crucial and should just be something that relates to your offer. This can be a picture of you giving

a speech whilst dressed professionally if you're selling a business-related offer, a picture of a stock chart if you're selling a trading offer, or a picture of a mother and child looking happy if you're selling a parental consulting offer. You get the picture, no pun intended.

Aside from those elements, the only others you'll add will be a button below the headline, and another below the bullet points. These, when clicked, will bring up a pop-up form that will collect the name, email and phone number of the prospect. When submitted, they'll be automatically redirected to the VSL page, where they'll then watch your "free training".

Here's an example of the opt-in I used in my e-learning company:

Believe it or not, I made this in January 2020 and literally did not change it once in over three years. This opt-in is responsible for over $15,000,000 in sales and more than 2,000,000 people have viewed it as of me writing this book. If you are in the trading niche, it's highly likely you've seen it yourself if you've ever clicked one of the ads I used to run.

VSL page

On this page, you'll simply have two things:

1. Your VSL or webinar.
2. A button below this where the viewer can either proceed to book a call with you if you're operating a "book a call" or webinar funnel that proceeds with a sales call; or proceed to a written sales page if you're running a webinar funnel that goes direct to purchase instead of requiring a sales call.

This is the VSL page I used in my e-learning company.

Schedule page or sales page

On this page, you'll do only one thing, which is either to insert your calendar so that prospects can choose a day and a time to speak with you if you're operating a book-a-call funnel or a webinar funnel that proceeds with a sales call, or you'll have a

This is the schedule page
I used in my e-learning company.

written sales page if you're running a webinar funnel that goes direct-to-purchase instead of requiring a sales call.

Thank-you page

On this page, you'll do two things:

1. You'll produce a short video that thanks the prospect for booking, or purchasing, along with any further steps they need to take, for example "Look out for an email with your Zoom link, and don't forget to attend with a pen and a piece of paper so you can take notes." Or "Look out for program access in your email inbox now," if they've just made a purchase.

This is the thank-you page I used in my e-learning company.

2. You'll share previous client successes in the form of reviews, testimonials or even client interviews to reaffirm that they've made a great decision by either booking a call, or purchasing, along with any other proof you can provide that what you do will work for them and get them amazing results. This is to get them excited for their upcoming call with you, or about the purchase they just made.

What's the underlying purpose of each page?

The purpose of each page is simply to make someone take the next step in your funnel, whether that's providing their contact details, booking a call or purchasing a webinar place.

The purpose only changes once they reach the thank-you page, which is designed to prepare them for the call or webinar and make them feel excited.

Dropping knowledge: troubleshooting low call show-up rates

In the online education industry, a good show-up rate to a call is 55 per cent. If you are achieving this, or above this, then you are doing something right and it's highly likely that your offer, your promise and your niche are all in alignment.

If you're below this rate, however, you're doing something wrong, or the niche you've chosen may not be one suited to the type of funnel you've set up – a good way to test this would be to swap your current funnel, like a sales call funnel, for one of the other options (a webinar or written sales page) and see if that makes the difference.

Sometimes it's not the type of funnel though, but your content itself. In my experience when call show-up rates are 35 per cent or lower, it's usually down to one of three things:

- A VSL that isn't compelling enough or is too long.
- A "thank-you" page that isn't compelling enough.
- A lack of reminder emails and SMS messages to remind the prospect of their upcoming call.

- A lack of trust, i.e. your content does not build enough trust and rapport for the prospect to want to follow-through on attending their call.

Point number three might sound simple – and it is – so it's a good place to start if your call show-up rates are lower than you'd like.

Thankfully, a low show-rate can very much be fixed in almost all cases, so please do not go throwing away your funnel or worse, niche-hopping. That is almost never the answer.

The $15,000,000 sales script

Sales is not magic. It's human nature. It's not something to be scared of. When you conduct a sales call all you are doing is having a fun conversation with someone who, because of the way we've built our sales process and funnel, is interested in how you might be able to help them. It really is that simple. Like I said in the previous chapter, sales may have a negative connotation attached to it, but it needn't. It's nothing more than a value-led conversation between a person who has a problem and needs help, and a person who is able to provide the specific help needed.

In this chapter, I'll share the exact, word-for-word sales script from my e-learning company that is responsible for turning thousands of prospects into paying customers like clockwork, in a repeatable, predictable and sustainable manner. This script is responsible for over $15,000,000 in sales. I'll explain everything from the different sections of the script and why we ask certain questions, to why the script is laid out in a specific order and how we remove objections before going anywhere near asking for a sale.

The script I'm about to talk you through is written, and conducted, in a very specific order based on human psychology. It's designed to trigger different emotions and beliefs, in a specific order, that results in the prospect feeling a want, and a need, to buy now, without waiting, in order to bridge a gap between being stuck with their current problem, and solving it. In making a purchase, your prospect believes they will achieve their desired outcome soon after buying your offer and receiving your help.

All you need to do is simply ask a certain set of questions, in a specific order, and believe me, people will simply buy from you. They really will. How? Because you will trigger the necessary emotions within them, and they will feel – within themselves, and by their own choice and conclusion – the need to buy from you based on the beliefs your questions have caused them to instil within themselves.

This flowchart sets out each part of the script and what I'll do now is share each section and its associated questions with you while explaining *why* this works so well.

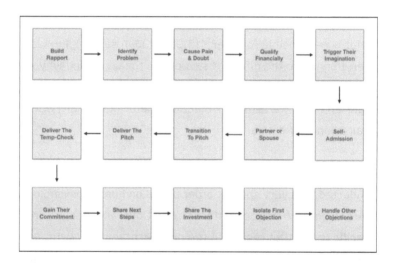

Build rapport

This is where you'll say hello and provide some gentle introductory words of welcome. No more than 60 seconds. Why? So that you feel comfortable together.

> "Hey [name], how's it going? Where are you calling from today? Do you have a pen and a piece of paper handy? Is your phone on silent? Just to check, do you have an hour or so set aside for the call today? Alright, well we can go ahead and dive in if you like?"

Identify problem

This is where you'll understand whether you can help the person or not, by asking them questions about their background, what they've already tried, and so on. Why? Because if they don't have a problem, they don't need our help and the call is useless – they will never buy from us. If there is no clear problem that they need to solve, politely end the call.

> "OK, so I just want to start by asking some questions about your background in [industry or niche] and what the journey has been like so far. If it sounds like we can help, and if it sounds like we're a good fit to work together, we can take it from there. Sound good? Great, so firstly I just want to ask, what brings you to the call today? What was it about [what brought them here] that stood out to you exactly? Talk to me about your background in [industry or

niche]. How's it all been so far? Have you had any specific education within it, or a coach or a mentor or anything?"

Cause pain and doubt

This is where you'll ask questions that help the prospect to reaffirm that they do in fact need help, along with going deeper on what else they've tried, why it failed, and why they're here now with you on the call. Why? Again, the prospect has no need to buy from us if they feel they can achieve success on their own. This section reaffirms their problem and has them tell us why they need our help.

> "What would you say is holding you back from achieving [goal, or solving problem] specifically? What don't you like about [plug in what they've just said]? Do you currently have a strategy, process or road map for achieving [goal, or solving problem]? Are you keeping track of your results? The fact you've taken the time to book in, and attend this call, tell me that maybe there's something missing, or standing in the way of your [goal]. So I guess, how does your ideal situation compare to what you're experiencing now? What's preventing you from getting to [goal, or solving problem]? OK, I understand, so it sounds like your biggest problems are [insert what they've told you]. Would you agree with that?"

Qualify financially

This is where you'll understand their financial circumstances, so that you can decide whether they are able to commit to purchasing your offer or not. If they cannot afford it, you will end the call here to save both their time and your own. Why? Your offer costs money. If they do not have the purchasing power to buy, we unfortunately cannot help them. If your offer is of a more personal nature, such as a service to help someone stop drinking, you would be less direct in your questioning over the prospect's finances than I set out in this script. Instead you can qualify them by asking questions about how much they spend on alcohol per week, for example.

> "OK I understand, and can I run a personal question by you? What's the impact been financially so far? Are you building upwards towards your monetary goals, or falling backwards away from them? OK, and what's causing you to move backwards and lose money? And what is it you're currently doing career-wise again? Are you happy in the role? Why not? Have you been building up any savings to use towards [achieving goal, or solving problem] at all? Have you begun deploying the savings as of yet, or? Oh, well why haven't you begun using the funds yet or perhaps invested in any education or coaching yet, if I can ask?"

Trigger their imagination

This is where you'll ask them questions about why they are doing what they're doing in the first place, along with what they hope to achieve in the future, triggering their imagination and getting them excited about what's to come when they've bought your offer. Why? If they are not excited about solving their problem, along with all of the great things that will happen once it's solved, they may be scared to commit and make a purchase. It's important that we help them see that everything they desire is on the other side of solving the problem. This also positions you as the trusted authority who can help them get there, increasing trust.

> "So, one thing I want to ask, and it might seem like a silly question, but why are you pursuing [niche] exactly? With that in mind, do you have a ball-park financial figure you'd like to achieve, let's say per month, or per year? Why that specific number though? Why not more, why not less? Understood, and what's the motivation behind all of this [achieving goal, or income, or solving problem]? OK, well let's say that you get your [problem solved, or ideal income], what do things look like then specifically?"

Self-admission

This is where you'll ask them questions in regards to why now is the time to make a change, or why they still haven't achieved their desired goal or reached success, along with getting them to admit to us that now is the time for change, and that they want to move forwards with solving their problem. Why? Because if they don't have a strong reason to act now, they won't. This will leave you with a "let me think about it" objection later in the call, and this will simply result in the prospect not solving their problem anytime soon. It's our job to help them to help themselves. We do this by asking them questions that allow them to admit to us that now is the time for them to get help and solve their problem once and for all.

> "OK, so I understand that you want to get to [goal, or solve problem] and I understand why you want to get there, so, I guess, what would you say is stopping you from getting there? Understood, and I always hesitate to ask this, but purely so we're on the same page, theoretically, what would happen if you didn't achieve [goal, or solve problem]? I understand. Well, one thing on my mind is, I guess, why now? Why not like, six months ago, or why not wait six months y'know? Why now? I see, and what would happen if you hit the pause button and just laid this aside for another year or something? Would you say that [achieving goal, or solving problem] has some urgency to it? Why, though?"

Partner or spouse

This is where you'll clarify whether they are the sole decision-maker or if there is, let's say, a business partner or a husband or wife who are part of their problem and their decision to solve it. If there is, we will temporarily pause the call here and reschedule at a time where their business partner or spouse can be present. Why? If they are not the sole decision-maker, this will leave you with a "let me run it by my partner" objection later in the call, and in most cases, you will never hear from them again. Because their partner has no idea of everything discussed on the call, they are likely to speak against making a decision now, and this will simply result in the prospect not solving their problem anytime soon. It's our job to conduct the full call with all parties present, and to help them to make a decision there and then, in order to trigger all of the important emotional responses needed for them to reach a "yes" or a "no" decision that serves them.

"You mentioned family briefly earlier, what does your partner think about this whole thing? Are they supportive of you pursuing this? Why, though? [or] Oh, I see, why not? Is there a business partner involved in your current venture? Do they support your decisions, or do you need to allow them to make key decisions on your behalf? I understand, and can I run one last personal question by you? Sometimes we find that certain clients like to involve their partner in their [insert your niche] journey, and kind of take on the venture together. Would that be the case with yourself, or is this purely your own pursuit? OK, got it.

So, when it comes to [insert your niche] and progressing towards your [goal, or solving problem] tis is solely your

own pursuit, you do the work, you make the decisions, everything? *if they say they must involve a partner, then say* I see, well in that case, let's pause the call here and let's re-book at a time when they can be present, because from a values perspective I would feel like I'm being disrespectful towards them by not having them be present whilst I cover everything. When would be a good day and time for you both to meet me back here to continue the discussion?"

Transition to pitch

This is where we have finished the discovery part of the call, and are about to explain, in our pitch, how we can help them solve their problem. However, if we jump straight into the explanation it can trigger sales resistance. To avoid this, we ask their permission to pitch them by asking if they'd like more information about how we can help. This removes sales resistance and allows us to deliver our pitch with confidence, because the prospect has asked us to do so.

"OK, well that's me done questions-wise. I've got a solid understanding of where you're at, and I definitely feel like we can help you. But yeah, where would you like to go from here? I mean, if you like, I can tell you more about what we do and how we can help, but yeah, you tell me where you want to go from here?"

Deliver the pitch

This is where you'll explain how you can help, the components of your online course, coaching program or mastermind, and any other important details that come with it. Why? They need a top-level breakdown of what they'll have access to, and how you'll help them to achieve the success they desire.

In this section, you'll be delivering your pitch, which you'll write yourself, I'll explain how in the next chapter. The only questions you'll ask are some surface-level ones between the sections of your pitch, for example, "Does that sound like it would help you?" and perhaps "Does that make sense?" or even "Does this sound good to you so far?"

Deliver the temperature check

This is where, before sharing the price, you'll "temperature check" the prospect by asking them how they feel about everything on a scale of one to ten. If they give you a low number, this will reveal that you have not conducted a good call and have likely either rushed, or made mistakes. If they give you a high number, this will indicate that you have conducted a great call and they are ready to move ahead and take action. Why? After we give them the price, their mind may in some cases start racing, and they'll forget everything you've covered with them. By asking them to recount everything you've discussed, along with placing a direct number on how they feel about everything, you are able to hold them accountable later in the call if they become fearful of moving forwards.

"Great, so just curious here, but in terms of everything we've just covered there, how do you feel about this whole thing? OK, understood, and just to be totally transparent here, one thing that's really important to us is alignment. When you come in and work with us, we are genuinely rolling up the sleeves and jumping into the trenches with you. I mean we are all-in, so it's really important to us that you feel solid, that you feel 100 per cent on the process, do y'know what I mean? Absolutely, so on a scale of let's say one to ten, with one being like "not interested, don't feel like this is for me, see ya later" haha, and ten being like "this is exactly what I need, it sounds amazing, let's do it", where do you feel like you fall on the scale exactly?

If they say nine or above, move to the next section. If they say eight or below, then say Got it, and I appreciate your honesty on that. So, what would you say is stopping you from being like, an eight or a nine or a ten? *From there, handle their uncertainty as you would any other objection, then move to the next section*."

Gain their commitment and share next steps

This is where you'll now ask them, for a final time, if there is anything else that is causing them doubt, or if they have any other questions, or if they are "100 per cent in", thereby gaining their full commitment to moving forwards with you. When they say yes, you'll then share the next steps such as covering pricing, enrolment and starting to work together. If they say no, you'll simply ask them why and reassure them, holding them accountable to everything they've covered with you thus far.

"Amazing, well with that said, just before we get into pricing and all of that stuff, is there anything else that's stopping you from being like, a 100 per cent certain here on feeling like the process and everything we've covered is what you need to [solve problem, or remove pain] that you mentioned earlier? Got it, so if I'm hearing you correctly, you're a 100 per cent in?"

Share the investment

This is where you'll share the price of your offer with them, and recap what they'll have access to. Why? It's important to share the price and then recap the features and contents of your offer so that they can tie the value together, pairing the price with all of the amazing ways in which you're about to help them. This will reduce their fear of purchasing because they will understand everything they are paying for, and how much it will help them.

> "Alright, sounds good. Well we've covered all of the program contents, all your questions are answered, you're a 100 per cent in, so what's next? I guess the next step is to cover pricing and all of that stuff, but yeah, you tell me where you wanna go next? No worries, so the program is just $8,000 and for that, you get full access to [insert contents] and also [insert coaching] and I've even added in [insert resources] for you too, that are all blueprinted and pretty much all "copy-paste" to save you time and hard work, if that makes sense. Also, you've got access for life, so there's no upgrades or extras to buy, either. So, that's the costing structure and everything you'll have access to. How do you feel about it all?"

Isolate the first objection

Most people will, at this stage – as long as you have properly conducted the call and followed each section in order – buy your program. The few who do not buy immediately are likely to give you an objection, which may be price, terms, needing to "think about it", or "speak to their partner", or similar. This is to be expected, it's natural to be nervous when making a life-changing decision. In order to handle it properly, we must isolate it by first calming them down by acknowledging you understand, and then asking them the questions that I've laid out below. Why? This will help to relieve their stress or worry and realign them on why they are on the phone with us in the first place, along with all of the great things that are to come when their problem is solved.

> "No problem, and I can appreciate that. Now, for a second, let's just pretend that money is out of the equation. How do you feel about the process specifically? I mean, do you feel like ultimately this is what you need to [solve problem]? OK, got it. So to be clear, if the program was free, I get the feeling you'd just be in right now, right? Understood, so price is the only thing holding you back? *If yes, discuss a payment plan or a small discount. If no, isolate the real objection and address it*."

Handle other objections

This is where we slowly converse with them about anything else that's on their mind, respectfully allaying their concerns, addressing anything they're unsure of and answering any questions they may have. Why? Here, we just want to make them feel happy, comfortable and ready to move forward with confidence so that we can help them.

"No problem, I hear you. And can I ask you an honest question on that? You've said that [insert objection] and when you say that, what do you mean specifically? OK, I understand. Is there a way that I can help to address that for you, I mean, is there something we didn't cover together? OK, got it. Well, is there anything I can do, or show you, or walk you through that would make joining today a possibility for you? Are there any other options or avenues you'd be open to exploring or walking through together in order for you to be able to [solve problem, or remove pain] like you said you wanted and needed to earlier in the call? You told me earlier that you wanted to [solve problem, or remove pain] and you also said that it needs to happen now, because [insert what they said]. So, I would be out of integrity with myself if I let you off this call without helping you to [solve problem, or remove pain] because I know that what we have here is the answer. So with that said, how can we make this work for you?"

It is that simple. I can almost guarantee that if you read through those questions, calmly and in order, people will buy from you. That said, it's important to be realistic – not every person will buy because not every person you speak to will be at the top of the buying triangle. A reasonable closing ratio is in the 20 to 30 per cent range, depending on the strength of your offer, the price of your offer and your sales and people skills.

Download a clone of our $15,000,000 script at:

www.howtotenmillion.com/resources

Removing objections

An objection is a reason (often untrue) for the prospect not to buy there and then with you on the call. The most common objections are:

1. "I need to think about it."
2. "I need to run it by my wife [or partner]."
3. "I can't afford it."

The first two objections usually mean either:

1. "I don't want to buy, but I'm scared to offend you by saying no to you, so instead I'll lie to you and then dodge your follow-up calls."
2. "There's a question stopping me from buying, but I don't dare ask it, because I feel like after an hour on the phone

with you, I should have asked it earlier and I don't want to look like an idiot, I just want to get off the phone."

The third objection usually means either:

1. "I don't want to buy, but I'm scared to offend you by saying no to you, so instead I'll lie to you and then dodge your follow-up calls."
2. "I think I can find this cheaper elsewhere."
3. "I think I can do it by myself."

Of course, in some cases it may be that they genuinely cannot afford it and you should offer them payment terms, for example a payment plan of some kind, or a small discount as a helping hand to allow them to make the purchase feasible.

More often than not though, an objection is a "smokescreen", as my sales manager Alex likes to say. So how do we prevent objections from arising? It's simple, we ask questions that remove them within the discovery part of a call – as you can see in the script I've just shared with you.

This is an integrity-led way of selling, because we do not push or tell people, we simply ask them leading questions that allow them to reach the right conclusion for them. Every once in a while, a prospect will say, "Actually, I'm not looking to buy anything right now, I'm just shopping around," and that is OK. If that is their truth, then at this stage, working with them may not be right for them.

Nonetheless, I would then ask, "I understand, and why is that, if you don't mind me asking? Is it not important to you to solve [problem or pain]?" and based on their answer, I may then also ask, "Do you feel you need any help at all with [problem or pain] because if not, that's OK and we'll just end the call now, seeing as you don't need any help." This will do one of two things – either they'll tell you that they do not need help and you'll politely end the call, or it will trigger the prospect and lead them to admit that, actually, they do need help, in which case you can examine why using the questions I've already shared.

In rare cases, even if you follow my script to the letter, these objections will still come up. Handling them is as simple as three words: "You told me...".

These three words instantly place the prospect back within their own words from earlier, and whilst this can be uncomfortable, it is necessary so that we can provide the value that the prospect is here to receive. After all, they booked the call for a reason and they need your help, so if you do not close them, you have let them down and have not served them.

Imagine if a patient said to a doctor, "Listen, the medicine you're prescribing sounds good, and I do need it, but I'm scared of needles, so I'll give the medicine a miss." Then, imagine if the doctor replied, "Yeah, that's fair enough that you're scared. Most people are when it comes to big decisions. Let's give it a miss then, and I'll bring flowers to your funeral, so no worries. Bye!"

Your prospect is the patient. You are the doctor. Do not let them down. They would not have booked a call and taken the time to attend, which in itself is a huge step, if they did not need your help. They need your prescription, your offer, the help and the value that your product or service provides. Yes, they might be scared or nervous, but I hope, for the sake of your personal fulfilment, the value you have to offer to the world, and your financial future, that you won't let them down.

Scripts for objection handling

I'd be hard pressed to fully explain how to handle objections inside a book alone, but to add as much value as possible for you I want to give you just one or two techniques to handle objections like a pro. The following, if said correctly and fluently, will help you to get prospects off the fence, and help people overcome their uncertainties and invest in themselves.

"I need to think about it". Say to them:

> "I hear you, and I can appreciate that. Now, for a second, let's just pretend that money is out of the equation, OK. How do you feel about the process here specifically? Do you feel like ultimately, it's what you need to get those problems that we laid out earlier solved, or?
>
> OK, got it, so just to be clear, it sounds like you're not in a "should" I do this place where you're going back and forth on if this is the best next step for you, it sounds like your

more in a "how" can I do this place, where you're 100 per cent in, it's just a matter of covering a few different thoughts that are going around in your mind right now, and then when that's done, you'd be in?

I hear you, that makes complete sense and thanks for sharing that that's the case. Much appreciated. And what are those specific thoughts, or questions, or doubts that are standing in the way of you doing this would you say?"

"It's hard to say exactly. I really just need to think about it." If the prospect still won't open up, then at this stage, here's a method I created that removes the objection in many cases. You must, however, act with confidence. What I'm about to share is responsible for six if not seven figures in sales by me and my coaching clients who I've taught this to. Say, and do, this:

"No worries at all, I respect that. Well I tell you what, I'm all out of coffee here so let me go and make another cup, I'll be about five or six minutes, so you go ahead and think everything through and we'll catch up when I'm back. Be back in a sec."

Then, stand straight up and walk out of the room. It's critical that you do not ask for permission or the prospect will simply tell you no, they must leave the call to think things through which, as we know, is a lie nine times out of ten. Whereas if you say this confidently and fluently, and walk straight out of the room, they will have no time to object and will be left with time to think things through, removing the objection entirely.

Caveat; You must speak confidently and fluently, acting with respect and the prospect's best intentions in mind, whilst giving them no time to offer a rebuttal. Do not hesitate or they will stop you from leaving. When done correctly, this technique is magic.

Please note, some prospects will put the phone down or exit the Zoom call before you return because they know that they are lying and they're embarrassed by the fact that they do not have a rebuttal to provide you with now that they have had time to "think about it". This is called a logic-trap. They cannot logically give the objection again because they've been given adequate time to think about it. So the only outcome from here is to either make up another objection, drop off the call, or buy.

When you get back after waiting for at least five straight minutes, then say this:

"Ahh, there we go. Awesome. Anyway, how did the thinking go?"

If, at this stage, they create a new objection, then say this:

"I hear you, and that's no problem at all. Hey, let's level with each other here because earlier in the call, you said you were 100 per cent in. Now you're telling me you have [objection]. Let's stay open and transparent so I can best help you: What's really going on here?"

You have to say this in a calm, genuinely curious manner. If you say it with a tone that comes across as angry or it seems like you're interrogating them, their guard will go up and it's all over. I once heard the correct tonality to use here described as the "curious old man" tone. If you say this part calmly, and with curiosity and openness, the prospect will begin to open up, share their genuine concerns or questions if they have them, and you can help them understand that buying will help to get them to where they want to go.

From there, if they still won't open up, then say this:

"Understood, and look, if this isn't something you want to do, you can absolutely say "no" here and we can close off the call, no problem at all. This call is all about you and getting your problems solved, that's why we're here, isn't it? But we can't do that unless we're straight with each other. And at the moment, you're holding something back that's preventing us from getting your problems solved, so again, let's level with each other here. What's the problem or the doubt? Let's cover it together.

One thing that's important to me is keeping my word and I'm sure you're the same, right, and if I let you think about it, I have to let everyone think about it. And before you know it, I'm filling up my calendar with people who are all thinking about it, but no-one is getting their problems solved which is the reason we're here in the first place. So again [name], if it's a "yes" then I'd love to help you and work with you. If it's a "no" we'll jump off the call and you can go back to the same struggles that prompted you to book this call in the first place. But let's not leave this on a "maybe" because that doesn't serve you. So, which of those two options – get the problems solved, or continue struggling with the things that brought you here in the first place – makes the most sense to you?"

At this stage, and if said correctly, most prospects will finally come to realise that you won't give up on them, and that the correct path forwards to ensure they get the result they desire is to buy from you. However, if they do not, then say this following their new objection:

"No problem, and can I share something with you? [pause]. Awesome, and here's the thing. I actually keep a log of all of these calls and their outcomes and I can tell you that statistically, 93 per cent of people who've asked me to reschedule or told me they'll pay later, they never come on-board. 93 per cent of people. Imagine if I rebooked all of those people on my calendar, or I tried to keep track of them all. It's just not possible, right? So, to show you and your time the most respect possible, let's level with each other here. Is this a "yes", like you said it was earlier when you said you were 100 per cent in, or is it a "no", and you'd prefer to carry on struggling on your own, which you said earlier that you were against?"

At this stage, we've done everything we can to help them reach a 'yes' or a 'no' decision and pushing any harder can begin to get distasteful. If they say 'yes' then take the payment and enrol them. If they say 'no' then politely end the call. If they still object, either book in a follow up if you choose to, or politely end the call.

"I need to speak to my partner" – Say to them:

"No problem. I respect that, and aside from running it by your partner, just so we're on the same page here, you're 100 per cent in and you absolutely want to do this, right? Great, so from your side, this is a straight up yes let's go?

Awesome, well that's really great to hear, and why do you feel so strongly about doing this specifically? Understood. And, when you run this by your partner, what do you think they'll say?

OK, and what if they say no? [pause] Got it, again, no problem. In fact I actually had another client of ours who said the same thing last week and they actually took it to their partner and said to them "I'm thinking of investing in a mechanical trading program, y'know, R-multiple this, risk-percentage that, annual-yield this, and in the end their partner just said to them 'Look, you know I don't understand any of this stuff. As my husband, I trust you. You've spoken to them, you do what you think is best for us' because, let's face it, not many people who aren't involved in trading know the in's and out's of mechanical trading, right? [make a joke out of it so the prospect laughs].

Haha, exactly, right. So do you think your partner would say something similar and not really understand the in's and out's of all of the mumbo jumbo, and just trust your decision-making? Or do they need to jump on a call with us both maybe tomorrow or the next day, so that I can run them through how it all works myself?

Sounds good. Well with that said, we can go ahead and get you started if you like?"

At this stage, you've aligned them with their partner's trust and, in a light hearted manner, have made your first swing at a close by saying "we can go ahead and get you started if you like". At this stage, many people will buy your program. If, however, they're still not sold, then say this:

"No worries at all. Well look, there is one thing I can do to completely remove any worry you have here and seeing as you've told me you're 100 per cent in, I know it's going to be perfect for you, so let's do this. We'll get you enrolled right now, and if your partner says no when you run this by them later on, I'll give you my personal phone number and my email address and you can drop me a call and I'll just refund you immediately, no questions asked. And that way, if it's a "no", then no worries you have the money back, and if it's a "yes" you're already enrolled and progressing through the program content. Win-win. And for your peace of mind I'll also give you that in writing, too. I'll get that over for you right now and we'll get you started. What's your email?"

Can you see here how, similar to the coffee-walk away technique I shared earlier, we do not ask for permission. We simply ask for their email, presuming that they'll accept the no-brainer proposition. After all, all risk is removed. If their partner says "no" we've committed to refund them, so they either love the program, or get their money back. Who could possibly say no to this? If, however, they do push back, then say this:

"I'm confused... you told me you were 10/10, you absolutely want to do this, and I'm letting you into the full program with literally, absolutely, zero risk. If your partner says "no", you not only get a refund, but you'll have even gotten value from the day or two you'll have had inside the program. Plus you have my promise to you in writing along with my number and my email address... What's really going on here?"

At this stage, we've made buying from us a no-brainer, because we've removed all risk for them by offering an 'any reason' refund if their partner is not happy about their decision to enrol. If they still won't budge, this reveals to us that they are not a buyer, or that they are highly sceptical and we need to build more trust before they're able to commit.

Pushing any harder at this stage can, again, begin to get distasteful. If they say "yes" then take the payment and enrol them. If they say "no" then politely end the call. If they still object, either book in a follow up if you choose to, or politely end the call.

"I can't afford it" – Say to them:

> "I hear you, and I can appreciate that. Now, for a second, let's just pretend that money is out of the equation, OK? How do you feel about the process here specifically? Do you feel like ultimately, it's what you need to get those problems that we laid out earlier solved?
>
> OK, got it, so just to be clear, you're not in a "should" I do this place where you're going back and forth on if this is the best next step for you, it sounds like your more in a "how" can I do this place, where you're 100 per cent in, it's just a matter of sorting the money side of things out, and then you're ready to go, right?
>
> Awesome, well if you're 100 per cent in and you want to do this, but it's just the money side of things that needs sorting out, let's get creative here. How can we make this work for you? Do you perhaps have a credit card we could

lean on, or maybe we could discuss a payment plan of some sort. You lead the way, what do you think we could do to get this solved together in a way that will work for you?"

At this stage, get creative and work out a way for them to be able to afford to enrol. If you're able to offer a discount of some sort, that can help. Or if you offer payment plans, run them through these, and then enrol them.

Writing your pitch

Writing a pitch is simple. All you need to do is identify two to three pillars of your offer. These are two or three key selling-points, or unique aspects, that your offer will use to solve the person's pain or problem.

Within my e-learning company, they were:

1. An explanation of how simple and effective our 'mechanical rules' are, and how they work.
2. How we use statistical data to ensure that the strategies are profitable and proven.
3. How we work hard to support and hand-hold our clients.

Once you've decided on your two or three pillars, simply write out a paragraph explaining each and then place a "recognition" question between each one. Here's an example, taken directly from the pitch me and my sales team used to use.

Pillar one: So, unlike most other strategies out there that tell you roughly what to do and then leave you to guess at the rest, what we do differently is we use an actual set of step-by-step rules that tell us exactly what to do at all times. Now, the rules are based on just price itself, so no indicators, no analysis, no reading the news or anything, and to help you understand how they work, would it help if I shared a quick hypothetical example of a trade, just to kind of paint the picture for you? *wait for them to say yes, and give you permission to move forwards*.

No worries, so let's say, you might discover that on 'x' market, let's say a currency market, at 11:00am every day, a special and specific candlestick forms based on our predetermined statistical data, which is in the training for you, that tells us where to buy, where to sell, where to place a stop-loss and a profit-target, everything is black and white and entirely rule-based. We just await the specific candlestick that you'll learn in the training content and use it as a reference point. In other words, the market directs us, instead of us using emotion to direct the market, so to speak, which simplifies the whole trading process and removes discretion entirely.

Recognition question: *Does that make sense? And would that level of clarity help you?*

Pillar two: Awesome. Now, within the program itself, you'll learn how to understand and identify these unique points within the markets, and you'll also be handed the statistical data that proves, as a mathematical fact, that what you're doing works and is, historically, a uniquely profitable way to trade financial markets. You can also take this data and unpack it, and even rebuild it for yourself using a method called back-testing, so that you can "see inside" the strategies and get a feel for how each trade often plays out.

Recognition question: *Would that level of clarity and proof bring more peace of mind for you?*

Pillar three: Fantastic to hear. And thirdly, a core element of what we do is the support and coaching we provide. This helps to hold you accountable, and reduce and remove mistakes, and also to help you even construct your own strategies in the future. We do this in two ways. One is via weekly group coaching, and two is via individual one-to-one coaching calls that you can book in with a dedicated support rep that we provide uniquely to you so that whatever you need, whenever you need it, we're all right behind you every step of the way.

Recognition question: *Have you ever had support at such a level before? Would it help, do you think?*

When you've done that – specific to your own offer, niche and deliverables – you've crafted your pitch. I suggest rehearsing it a few times, along with your whole script, before you begin taking live sales calls, just so that it feels natural when you deliver it all.

Action points

Your next step from here is to rewrite all of the questions included in the sales script I shared to suit your offer. The key is to ensure they make sense in respect to your deliverables and niche. Once you've got your script sorted, it's time to write your custom pitch.

Why don't you pause here and start writing your sales script and pitch? Once you have both of these elements, you can combine them into a fully-fledged professional sales script, ready to read during your sales calls. Very soon, the money will begin to flood in for you.

Although I discussed filtering and qualifying people during your sales calls, there is also a technique you can use to filter out unsuitable prospects before they get in front of you – it's called funnel friction...

Chapter 8

Funnel Friction and Survey Mathematics

Funnel friction is a technique to significantly reduce the number of unqualified people making it to your sales calls, and to increase the volume of sales calls you have in your calendar – the two most common problems people face once they have a sales funnel up and running.

In short, funnel friction is a way to engineer each step of the sales process to either add qualification, or take away qualification, from your leads. If you are speaking to people who are broke or who do not have the problem you solve, you need to *increase* the amount of friction in your sales funnel. If you are only speaking to one or two people a week, you need to *reduce* the amount of friction in your sales funnel.

The best ways to increase friction are:

- Be more direct in your ads, by using very specific, targeted language to call out only the specific people you want to click, and repel those you don't want to speak to.
- Take the same targeted and specific approach on the opt-in page, and within your VSL.
- Add either more questions, or more targeted and specific questions, to your call booking survey.
- By increasing friction, you will decrease funnel throughput. In other words, fewer people will flow in, and through, the funnel.

Here, it's likely that prospects who book calls will be more interested, and more qualified, meaning whilst you may have fewer calls and leads, you'll almost certainly experience a higher call closing rate.

To reduce friction, you essentially do the opposite:

- Be less direct and more broad in your ads, and do not call out specific people who you want to click.
- Use less targeted, less specific language.
- Be less exact on your opt-in page, and also within your VSL.
- Either remove questions or make your questions less targeted and specific on your call booking survey.

By reducing friction, you will increase funnel throughput, so more people will flow in, and through, the funnel. However, it's likely that the prospects you attract will be less interested, and less qualified. Although you can still make sales with these leads, as you will have more of them, you'll need a higher volume of calls to make up for a likely lower call closing rate.

The magic of survey mathematics

I invented survey mathematics within my e-learning company and it will, undoubtedly, make you more sales and give you a huge advantage over any competitors – as long as they don't get their hands on this book, that is! No-one does this because it's difficult and takes time, and thought. However, if you do it, you will make more money, save time, and be able to scale your business further and faster than most other business owners.

In general, when you begin your business and are running a sales call funnel, you'll take all the calls you get. You might cancel the odd call based on survey answers – such as from those who it's obvious almost certainly can't afford your program. But that will still leave you with a lot of calls – and a lot of occasions when you think, *what a waste of time that call was. They were far from qualified and sucked my energy away from the other good calls I have coming up. I wish I'd known earlier so I could have avoided that call.*

Survey mathematics can stop that for good.

Dropping knowledge: setting up survey mathematics

There are three steps to this process.

Step one is to make sure that your survey questions are multiple choice, not written answers. This is so that we can quantify the data we collect. We cannot quantify written answers as they vary too widely. Obviously, when it comes to questions like "what is your current job title or occupation", we must leave this as a text field, but for all other questions – such as income, age or any "yes" or "no" question – use radio buttons where the prospect can only select one answer.

Step two is to take 250 calls, only cancelling the obviously terrible surveys you receive – the ones that in almost all cases do not, and cannot, close. Aside from those, accept and take every other call that is booked, until you've completed 250 calls in total.

Step three is to create a spreadsheet – like the one that follows – that has a tab for each question, and each answer. For example, this sheet is open on the tab that lists every person who, when they booked a call, selected that they had a $1,000 to $2,000 income.

Once you have everything set up, you can make the magic happen. Once you have a list of people who selected a certain answer, you check your online store to see how many of them bought, and how much total sales revenue you brought in from this group of prospects.

You then calculate your cost per taken call. To get this number, you take your advertising spend across one full month, and divide it by how many calls you took that month.

I know this might sound complicated, but stay with me. I am about to make you millions of dollars.

Here's a hypothetical example to bring it to life. We're sticking with the people who told us they had an income of $1,000 to $2,000:

- We spent $20,000 on ads to essentially "buy" 50 taken calls ($400 per call).

- This brought in 10 sales, equalling $50,000 in total sales revenue ($5,000 per person).
- This resulted in a $30,000 profit, which is the $50,000 we made minus the $20,000 we spent acquiring those customers.

This tells us that if someone selects that they have an income of $1,000 to $2,000 we should prioritise their call because, mathematically, they are extremely profitable and these people are proven to buy our program. This is not opinion, it is mathematical fact, which we know from our data analysis – or our survey mathematics as I call it. We can now be certain that when a prospect books a call and selects this answer, regardless of their other answers, we should take the call.

This also works in reverse – so if you see that only two people out of 50 in the $0 to $500 income bracket bought your program, you would calculate that as a loss of $10,000 – $20,000 to acquire all 50 leads, minus the $10,000 you made from the two who did convert.

This tells us that if someone selects that they have an income of $0 to $500 we should not prioritise their calls and in fact cancel them because, mathematically, they are not profitable and these people do not buy our program. We can now be certain that when a prospect books a call and selects this answer, regardless of their other answers, we should cancel the call.

I suggest taking calls until you have at least a sample size of 50 calls for each answer. Ideally, you want 100 calls for each answer. This is because, in a small sample of calls, anything can happen. You might take five calls and close every one, or you might take 15 calls and close none. That's the nature of a small, random sample. Whereas in an accurate sample size of between 50 calls and 100 calls, this data is reliable, allowing you to know which survey answers are most likely to result in buyers.

There's nothing stopping you taking every call that gets booked, just in case, but using survey mathematics will save you time and energy. It makes you and your sales team far more efficient and it avoids those demoralising days when you have a string of terrible calls and make zero sales. Days like that can lead to doubt, emotional reactivity, bad decisions and wasted advertising spend. That's why survey mathematics is such a game-changer, because it maximises call quality and saves human time and energy. If you want to gain an edge over your competitors, this is one of the best methods you can use.

Action points

Once your sales funnel is set up, take a look at the quality of calls you're getting booked in and the number of sales you're making – do you need more or fewer calls in your diary? Apply the simple rules of funnel friction to make your sales pipeline more efficient quickly, and then turbo-charge it by bringing in survey mathematics. I know that collecting all that data will take time – but just think of the time and energy you'll save in the future by being able to be not only more selective with the sales calls you take, but more confident in your decisions too.

Chapter 9

Servicing Your Clients and Fulfilment Best Practices

In Chapter 3 I told you to never build a product before selling it – as I explained, it's essential to make sure there is demand for your product before you fully commit to it.

The biggest mistake in business is building a product before validating that people want to buy it. The way we validate our offer is by doing everything I've shared already in this book and using our marketing content, funnel and sales calls to gauge feedback from the marketplace.

These are the questions I ask myself (and answer) whenever I'm launching a new offer:

- How much organic content do we need to release before a sale is made?
- How much advertising spend does it cost to book a sales call?
- What type of prospect are we speaking to on our calls – do they have the pain or the problem that we solve?
- Are they financially qualified, and if not, what did they expect from our offer, and what kind of price point were they expecting?
- How much pain were they in, and what objections did they present us with, if any?

Once I have this data, I can then make changes if needed, whether that's to the ads, the funnel, the sales script or the offer itself. Or if everything is in alignment, I'll press on. Let's imagine your offer has taken off and you're making sales – now it's time to deliver.

At this stage, you might panic because you haven't created all your course content yet. Don't stress though. My recommendation is to coach your clients one-to-one via video calls, initially. You'll arrange two to three one-hour calls per week in a group setting and you'll teach them what they need to achieve the promised result or outcome – remember that the course you're delivering is based on something you're already an expert in. As you do this, you will use what you learn, along with what works best, to create your course content in the background.

I suggest building your course content in either sections, or in weeks. Personally I prefer sections, which I release to my clients one-by-one. I unlock each new section daily across a week, so that my clients can slowly and steadily build everything they need to create and release an offer that makes money for them extremely quickly and easily.

Alternatively, many courses I've invested in over the years have been delivered in weeks. This simply means your clients get content each week, which is designed to be viewed and acted upon in that timescale. There is no right or wrong choice between sections and weeks – the decision simply dictates how quickly you want your clients to progress through your material.

Minimum viable product (MVP)

Your MVP is the first version of your online course, coaching program or mastermind, and you'll create it within a couple of weeks of having your first coaching calls with your clients. At this stage, what you create will not be breathtaking. The intention is to have a viable product, and use the feedback from your initial clients to improve and iterate your product.

My recommendation is to sell five to ten people into your initial group coaching program and conduct two weeks of video calls with them. Use what you learn in these sessions to create a basic version of your online course. This simply has to be good enough to get your clients their desired result, but no more. No bells, no whistles – don't worry about fancy design or creating six to eight weeks of content at this stage.

Once you have your MVP, sell 50 to 100 people into this version of your course. Doing so will often add six figures to your bank balance, enabling you to hire a support rep or a coach, if required. This is when you start building a more in-depth version of your program. You might improve the audio quality, improve the design of the slides, film the videos in a studio with great camera equipment, make the course portal look more professional, and so on.

At this point, you have a great business. Your clients are happy, you're making great money, you have built a solid product that adds tremendous value. You can sell up to 1,000 more people into your program before you'll need to make any more iterations. Even at a lower price point of, say, $4,000 you'll be on the road towards making well in excess of seven figures.

Coaching architecture

In most cases, an online course plus once per week group coaching is enough. That's the baseline. It's difficult for me to prescribe what type of coaching architecture is right for your offer and niche without speaking to you first, but here are the main elements you can play with:

• Group coaching
• One-to-one coaching
• A client group i.e. a Facebook or Skool group
• A private client chat i.e. a Whatsapp chat or a Voxer chat.

I've listed those in order of the easiest to provide and least time consuming, to the most difficult and most time consuming. I'd also encourage you to keep fun in mind. If you hate speaking one-to-one with people, don't offer one-to-one coaching. If you love talking to a group, offer group coaching.

My e-learning company offered our program for $8,500, which included extensive course content, twice-weekly group coaching calls and three one-to-one coaching calls for each client to use at will with one of our in-house coaches.

This is likely more coaching than you need to provide, certainly initially. In most cases, one or two group calls per week – hosted via Zoom – are more than enough.

My advice is to architect your coaching based on what you feel your clients need to succeed. This also varies by niche and offer. Sometimes, people need more one-on-one support, sometimes they need none at all. A good way to decide what to offer for your clients is to ask, what would I want myself if I invested in this course, coaching program or mastermind? What type, and frequency, of coaching would I need to succeed and to get the promised result? Then, simply provide that for your clients.

If you're still unsure, my advice is to start simple. Group coaching alone is very effective and the group can add a lot of value. Make sure whatever you choose is also fun for you.

Also, don't forget that eventually you'll be able to hire coaches to help you, like I did. When I grew tired of providing one-to-one coaching and my passion for that deliverable faded, I simply hired my best client, Tom Wilson, to take over that side of my business. Four years later, he's still heading up the company's coaching department.

Pricing models

Value and unit economics are the two factors you'll use to decide on a price tag for your online course, coaching program or mastermind. Before we get into those though, here are a few examples of some existing offers to give you a benchmark.

- How to cut hair: $4K
- How to run ads: $5K
- How to produce music: $2.8K
- How to get six-pack abs: $5K
- How to read books faster: $2K
- How to become a closer: $10K
- How to take pictures of birds: $4K
- How to trade financial markets: $9K
- How to stop drinking alcohol: $8.5K
- How to stop smoking cannabis: $2.8K
- How to start a recruitment agency: $6.5K
- How to get a job selling software services: $10K
- How to talk to members of the opposite sex: $5K
- How to outsource the production of audiobooks: $10K
- How to have your children sleep through the night: $3.5K
- How to start an accounting or bookkeeping business: $2.8K
- How to identify and then resell popular online products: $5K
- How to outsource the production and operation of a faceless YouTube channel: $8.5K

I know what you're thinking, *are you serious? $4,000 to learn how to take pictures of birds? $10,000 to learn how to make audiobooks? Who is paying these prices, that's insane.* Until you're in the world of high-ticket offers – and if you've never invested this amount in your own education before – it can feel intimidating to see prices such as these. But I'd encourage you to see the value in these, rather than just the price tag.

$4,000 might seem steep to learn how to take pictures of birds. However, if you're a life-long bird and photography fanatic, who happens to have a high income – not to mention if you have aspirations of building a career doing this, with dreams of selling your photographs or starting your own studio or gallery – $4,000 is a no-brainer. When you truly understand the full story, the price suddenly feels like it's low.

Similarly, $10,000 might seem steep to learn how to create and sell audiobooks. However, when you've learned the skill and, in six months, you've been able to release so many audiobooks that your passive income via Audible each month is, let's say, $3,000 then you've gained a $36,000 per year income. And that's if you stop making additional audiobooks and just sit on the royalties – you might want to keep making more, thus pushing that income up. Again, the value now makes the price of the course seem low – the course is selling the ability to control, and scale, a passive income source as far as one would like, whilst creating valuable listening experiences for your customers, and also having fun in the process.

My point is that you need to consider the entire lifetime value that you are providing to your clients, and everything that comes with the skill that you teach and the awesome experiences that you are creating for them, when you're pricing your program. In many cases, when the skills you teach are used to their full

potential, they are worth many thousands of dollars to the right person.

Dropping knowledge: Pricing based on value

For products that provide the customer with an income, for example real estate investment, I usually suggest pricing the offer at around 20 per cent of the income that the customer can, on average, expect to earn within 12 months. This allows the customer to gain a great return on their investment, whilst making sure that you are fairly compensated for helping them.

So, if you're able to help someone make $50,000 within 12 months, then I suggest that you charge roughly $10,000 for this.

For products that do not provide the customer with an income, such as "how to take pictures of birds", I usually suggest pricing based on perceived value, whilst keeping unit economics in mind (I'll come to that shortly), and aligning this with the average income of your avatar.

In this case, people interested in wildlife photography tend to be relatively wealthy with a reasonable amount of disposable income. When running paid ads to an offer like this, I'd expect a typical cost-per-sale to be approximately $1,500 as an estimation. Therefore, we would need to charge $3,000 to make a 2x return on investment. This is both a great return, especially if achieved inside of any one month, and a more than acceptable price point based on the avatar.

Also remember the value of time – our most precious asset. Art forms such as painting, music and photography are incredibly fulfilling and fun, but they take time, skill and effort to learn. Don't underestimate the value of offering a program that allows someone to master an art form quickly.

The lesson is to charge appropriately if you are providing value for people.

It goes without saying that I cannot recommend an exact price for your offer in a book. I'd need to speak to you to understand your goals, whether you're using paid or organic traffic to acquire clients, and other variables.

One suggestion I do want to add here though is to consider not just an upfront fee, but either a fee plus a recurring subscription, or simply a recurring subscription. As an example, I currently provide one-to-one coaching to business owners who want help building and selling an offer, building a team, preparing a business for sale – essentially everything I've mastered over the last decade. I charge a monthly fee that varies based on the time-commitment the client wants from me, and I allow them to cancel at any time. They also get access to my online training course where I have documented every step of how to build and scale an eight-figure info business.

Some people work with me for just one month, some for six months or longer. My longest standing client has been with me for 14 months now. He has also attended my in-person mastermind event in Dubai twice and, in total, he has paid me over $110,000 so far. That is the power of a recurring fee rather than a one-time fee.

As you carry on providing value, you keep getting paid for it on an ongoing basis. Play with the pricing of your offering to achieve your goals.

I recently saw an offer priced at $30,000 to get access, plus $2,000 per month to keep access, to the private client group, the ever-evolving course-content and "any time" one-to-one coaching calls with the business owner and his team of sales and marketing experts. What a great offer and price.

Unit economics

Unit economics basically means the numbers required to sustain the successful, profitable, operation of a business.

As an example, I know that "buying" one booked sales call by running paid ads, typically costs around $50. Note the word "booked" call, not "taken" call. In the current online business landscape, I observe a typical show-up rate of around 55 per cent, which means on average you'll need to book two calls in order to take one call. So, if the average cost of a booked call is $50, that means it will cost around $500 to book ten sales calls. Let's say that five of those show up, at a 50 per cent show-rate, so it costs $250 to "take" five calls.

Now, let's imagine that you are new to sales calls and you only close one person at a price of $1,000 for your program. You have just spent $500 on paid ads in order to make $1,000 in return, leaving a profit of $500 and a 2x return on investment (ROI), which is a 100 per cent return because you've doubled your money.

Anyone who knows a thing or two about the world of investments knows that an average annual ROI in today's world is around seven per cent depending on the vehicle – the S&P 500 averages seven per cent per year, real estate averages six per cent per year. In the world of online education, however, a return of 100 per cent per week is not unheard of. In fact, if you speak to any successful e-learning founder who runs paid ads, they will almost certainly quote the fact that they make over 100 per cent, if not 200 per cent or higher ROI, per month – not per year; not per quarter. *Per month.*

At my e-learning company, we routinely produced a return of, on average, 160 per cent per month as a cash-return, and 270 per cent per month as a revenue-return. That was when we were spending over $150,000 per month on ads – so for every $1 we spent, we would make back $1.60 in cash and $2.80 in revenue. Every single month, like clockwork.

Put that in your pipe and smoke it, S&P 500.

If you get your unit economics right, which means your program price is high enough to enable you to make a profit based on your unique costs, you genuinely have a money-printing machine. I don't say that lightly. I truly mean it.

Look at the example I shared of our advertising tracking sheet from May 2023. That month, we spent $150,830 on ads and we returned 277 per cent in revenue and 160 per cent in cash, producing $574,812 in total sales volume.

How would you spend half a million dollars, made in a single month?

One number to pay attention to in that example is $973, which is our cost per sale. In other words, it costs us that amount to actually close a sale and gain a customer. That means that if the price of our program was $1,000 then we would make $27 profit per sale – that is not good. If you had a cost per sale of $973, what would you price your course, coaching program or mastermind at?

When you invest in my private business coaching program, you'll get access to a comprehensive training course which goes into all of this in much more detail. I've got a video which specifically breaks down the tracking sheet I've just shared a screenshot of, and all the metrics it contains. You can also download the sheet containing all of my data, so that you can not only see inside a multi-million dollar business, but also input your own numbers and let the inbuilt formulas highlight the good and bad parts of your funnel. This tool will instantly show you what to fix to enable you to make more money – and it's available exclusively to my coaching clients.

Our price point during that time was $8,500 for our front-end program, though not every sale was generated at the full amount because we also offered payment plans and, on occasion, a small discount of some sort in order to close a deal whilst on the first sales call with a prospect.

The key to unit economics is finding out what it costs you to make a sale – which will require you to invest money in paid ads to buy that data. Use that data to price your program efficiently in order to generate a profit. If you are unable to charge a high enough price on the front-end – which means for your primary product – then add a back-end product or service, also called an up-sell. This is a second, optional purchase that someone can make after becoming a customer, as I explained in Chapter 5.

We currently offer a $8,500 front-end online course, a back-end $7,000 online mastermind and a back-end $350 per month recurring software offer. This allows us to maximise how much money we make from each customer by adding value for them in three different ways. Typically, of the people who buy our front-end online course, 12 per cent will go on to buy the mastermind and 18 per cent will go on to buy the software, which maximises the "lifetime value" of each customer.

Coming back to unit economics, can you see now how important the price of your program is, if you want to scale? Speaking of scaling I should mention that the more you spend on ads, the higher your costs will be. Unfortunately this is the nature of the ad platforms, but nonetheless, you can still do very well even with a mid-tier price point of $3,000 to $4,000. However, if you scale far enough, you will either need to implement some kind of back-end offer, or raise the price of your main front-end offer.

But don't worry, you can scale to well over $250,000 per month, if not more, before the problem of rising costs rears its ugly head.

Sales up, expenses down

"Sales up, expenses down"

Nelson Peltz,
Billionaire Investor & Fund Manager

Believe it or not, it's that simple.

For a business to make money, it needs to make more sales (money in) than its expenses (money out). Nelson Peltz is what's known as an activist investor – someone who buys large stakes in public companies in order to gain control of them and have a say in how they are run. He then optimises the company to increase sales and reduce expenses to make the stock price go up. This makes him a profit on all of the shares he bought, and he then either sells his stock, making millions, or keeps the company in his portfolio of businesses that he and his firm own.

If you are starting a business, always keep this phrase in mind: sales up, expenses down. Keep your expenses as low as is feasible, and make as many sales as you're able to. If you follow the strategies and guidance I give to you in this book, you will almost certainly start and launch a profitable information business. If you run into bumps in the road however, nine times out of ten, the problem is either that expenses are too high, or sales are too low.

One way to quickly fix a profitability problem is by charging a higher price. I can't tell you how many "broken" offers I have fixed by simply having the offer owner increase their pricing. Another way to fix a profitability problem is by reducing expenses, of which there are many – lead cost, booked-call cost, cost per acquisition, sales rep commission, coaching costs, the owner's salary, and so on. Reducing these is not as challenging as you might imagine.

Lead cost: By improving your ads, opt-in or your lead magnet, lead cost will drop.

Booked-call cost: By improving your lead cost and your VSL or webinar, booked-call cost will drop.

Cost per acquisition: By improving your booked-call cost, or by better training your sales team, cost per acquisition will drop.

Coaching costs: By altering the length of coaching sessions that you provide, or by transitioning from one-to-one to group coaching, you may be able to renegotiate and lower the rates you pay your coaches, if necessary.

Owner's salary: Wait, you're paying yourself a salary when expenses are an issue? Get real. Stop that immediately, or at the very least reduce it to the absolute minimum so it covers just your basic monthly expenses.

I'll say it again. Sales up, expenses down.

That's how the big boys do it, that's how you'll do it, too.

Just do it

Feeling intimidated?

That's OK. No-one ever said that building a multi-million dollar business would be easy. I want to encourage you to simply take "massive, messy action". Write this down – finished is better than perfect. Most people never finish anything due to feeling the need for it to be "perfect", when in reality perfection does not exist. What good is something that never gets finished? You may as well have never started.

By not creating your offer, you are depriving people of the value you have to share with them. That is doing a disservice to the world. Whether you know it yet or not, you have unique talents, skills and knowledge that others would love to learn and will pay to learn. I ask that you take action on what you've learned so far and don't worry about it being perfect. Take massive, messy action!

Action points

Right now, just do one single thing. Put one foot in front of the other and take the first step. It can be anything. Just take action! Grab a pen and paper and brainstorm ideas for your offer. Or open a ClickFunnels account, import my funnel template from the following link and have fun making it your own. Or open a social media account that you'll use to acquire clients organically and start making valuable content. Or download my funnel tracking sheet from the following link and begin planning your pricing and costs.

Access all of the resources that I mention throughout this book, including funnel templates, pre-written scripts and other helpful done-for-you documents:

www.howtotenmillion.com/resources

It doesn't matter what you do right now. Just do something. Take the first step, take action.

"Just do it"

Phil Knight,
Founder of Nike

Download William's 16.4M Dollar Resources

Scan the QR Code Below

Part 2

Scaling Up

In this next part of the book, I'll be sharing the secrets behind scaling your online education business, or agency, to huge heights. These are the things that will give you an edge over the competition, allowing you to maximise sales and, in turn, your income.

I've learned these secrets whilst in the trenches on the battlefield. They are the strategies and tactics that have helped me to not only scale my e-learning company, but to also maintain that scale for years on end in a very efficient manner. I've never seen some of what I'm about to share with you talked about or documented elsewhere.

I suggest reading this next section alone, and keeping your notes secret. You won't want others to know this stuff, especially not your competitors. You're about to gain a severely unfair advantage and easily add six figures to your annual revenue.

Thank me later.

Chapter 10

Hidden Efficiency Techniques

If you are lucky enough to have either an email list or a social media following that includes people who could potentially buy your program, then you are sitting on a goldmine. Let's discuss how to instantly create sales by providing value to these people.

It's not uncommon for me to help someone who joins my business coaching program with an existing audience make five if not six figures within just days. Let me share an example, and then we'll cover the how, so that you can achieve the same.

Client story: Oliver Denyer – E-Commerce Coach

Oliver was my first-ever business coaching client. In fact, he inspired me to begin sharing everything I've learned, and to create and build my own program to help others like him to properly build and scale an online education business.

Oliver, if you ever read this book, thank you. You've helped me regain a sense of purpose and fulfilment that I had lost after selling my e-learning company.

During a mastermind that I used to be a part of – Dan Bradbury's financial literacy mastermind – Oliver heard Dan telling a story of my success. It resonated with him because he also ran an online education business, and he desperately wanted to scale, but he could not for the life of him break past $30,000 per month in sales.

Oliver messaged me via Instagram asking for my help. We agreed to speak once per week via Zoom for an hour. I began sharing all of the tips, tactics and strategies I'd used to grow my e-learning company up to over $800,000 per month in total sales revenue.

Within just nine days of our first call, Oliver had made $95,300 in cash. Not revenue, but cash-collected, using one of the efficiency techniques you'll learn later in this book – a re-offer. Not only that, but using my funnel metrics tracking sheet he could finally see his numbers clearly for the first time in three years of operating his business, which revealed the bottlenecks in his sales funnel, along with the precise amount of ad spend he needed to "pour in" to book the required

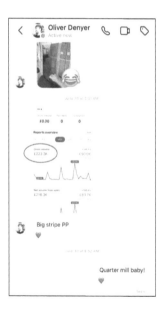

number of sales calls and, therefore, close the number of sales he needed to hit his $100,000 per month goal.

Just months later, by finally knowing his numbers and having control over the "cogs in the machine", he had sailed past his $100,000 target and had just wrapped up a $282,336 month – as you can see from that Instagram message on the final day of the month. This was his highest earning month to date, and he grew his total sales revenue by 840 per cent. It's a far cry from when he was stuck at monthly sales revenue of just $30,000.

Oliver is not a rare exception. I routinely help my business coaching clients achieve this level of success. If you have an email list or a social media following, again, you are sitting on a goldmine that could earn you four, five, even six figures in cash over the next few weeks, if not just days. There are several ways to unlock this goldmine. You could use the nine-word email I shared with you in Chapter 3, launch a re-offer (which I'll cover shortly), or run simple and low-cost retargeting ads. The aim is to send your audience into your sales funnel and encourage them to book calls, which usually results in instant sales. The best part is these leads are free, because you already have them on your list.

The power of email: dos and don'ts

There are a few key ways to use email addresses that you have collected:

1. Send those who have not bought from you yet "book a call" emails to generate sales calls, or even a webinar which can be live or pre-recorded, to generate sales calls.
2. Send them a re-offer to instantly generate sales revenue.
3. Send up-sell or down-sell offers to your existing customers to add additional value for them, perhaps offering them additional coaching, a mastermind or live event, or a software as just a few examples.
4. Send either your customers, those who have not bought from you yet, or both, affiliate offers sharing other high-value products or services from other companies whereby you earn a slice of the pie – usually around 25 to 50 per cent of the sale value – if they make a purchase. In fact, a year or so ago, I ran my first-ever affiliate promotion to my e-learning company's email list and generated almost a quarter of a million dollars, selling a $1,997 product at a commission of $997 per sale.
5. Build "contingency" streams for your sales funnel, where you essentially plug the holes that people fall through with specific emails that fire as people get stuck. For example, a specific email for people who see the opt-in, but who don't submit their info; another for people who submit their info, but who don't watch the video – you get the idea.
6. Those are things you should do. But what should you not do?

One big mistake I often see people making is formatting an email in a commercial manner, with text centred in the middle, banners, graphics and logos all over the place, fancy colours and, worse still, gimmicky subject lines like "brand new program, buy it now!".

This is a fast-track way to make people ignore your emails, unsubscribe from your list, and to trigger massive sales resistance that puts people off of you for good. There are two very simple ways to construct emails that people will open and read though:

Make sure they look exactly like a real email – plain text, aligned left, no fancy colours or logos.Use subject lines that look and feel real, for example;

"Hey [first name] is everything OK?" or "Just checking in, [first name]…" or "RE: Our call together".

I love using the "RE:" format as people always think it's a response to their communication which gives them a dopamine hit and spikes open rates. But you must make sure that your email is congruent with the subject line, or people will simply unsubscribe. Let me share three simple – but high engagement and high open rate – emails that I've used in the past to show you how easy this is.

Subject line:

RE: Our call together

Body copy:

Hey [first name],

It's Will from [company name].

I just realised you didn't book in your call with me about your [problem or pain that you solve]. Should we get it booked in this week? Let me share my calendar so you can pick a slot: [calendar link]

Just one thing, my calendar is almost full so please book in sharpish.

Chat to you soon [first name].

Simple, to-the-point, no BS and congruent with the subject line. That's a winning email. You can use this to book sales calls, and you can even resend it every four or five weeks as new people join your email list and others forget they've seen it in the past. I would, however, adjust the subject line a little, just to keep it fresh.

Subject line:

Hey [first name] is everything OK?

Body copy:

Hey [first name],

Is everything OK? Just asking because I saw you joined [name of your program] two weeks ago, but you didn't claim your invite to the [name of your mastermind up-sell]. We've only got two seats left right now, would you like one before they're all gone?

In the mastermind, you get [insert everything they get]. And no. there's no [things they hate]. In fact some of our most successful clients used the mastermind to dramatically boost their results. I want the same for you.

Let me know : -)

Again, it's simple, to-the-point, and just covers what needs to be covered in a non-salesy manner. I've added a tiny bit of scarcity by saying "we've only got two seats left" to increase urgency, and I've hinted at how our "most successful clients" join the mastermind, to trigger the feeling of, *if their most successful clients join it, maybe I should, too.* Humans are tribal animals, don't forget.

Subject line:

Just checking in [first name]

Body copy:

Hey [first name],

Just checking in because I noticed that you joined [name of your program] two weeks ago, but you didn't claim your invite to the [name of your mastermind up-sell]. We've only got two seats left right now, would you like one before they're all gone?

In the mastermind, you get [insert everything they get]. And no. there's no [things they hate]. In fact some of our most successful clients used the mastermind to dramatically boost their results. I want the same for you.

Let me know : -)

Here, I've re-used the previous email and added a re-frame to it. I've changed the subject line so it feels like a new email and I've also kept congruence between the subject line and the email. Apart from the lead-in to the email, it's exactly the same. You'd do this in order to plug your mastermind for a second time, to the same customers, but perhaps four weeks later.

It's that simple. No need for any gimmicks or complexity. Just talk like a human, keep the subject lines nice, fun and natural, stay away from anything commercial looking, and you'll be golden. Email truly is where the money is made much of the time. You can use it to make sales using a re-offer, to offer up-sells or down-sells to leads or customers, or to book sales calls, the whole shebang.

Speaking of re-offers, let's cover those next.

The $243,000 re-offer

That's how much my e-learning company made in an average year from sending out re-offers to our database of email leads who had not yet bought our main program. A re-offer is just that – it's making an offer for the second time, or "re" offering someone your product or service. Pretty nifty, right?

The great thing about re-offers is that it truly is free money. You have already paid for the lead. They are on your email list, but they are not booking a sales call with you and are ignoring your "book a call" emails. They are refusing to buy your main program for whatever reason. Then "ping" they receive a re-offer email and finally buy from you.

What do they buy? Usually a re-offer will be for your main program, but at a much more affordable price – a price that does not require a sales call. What price requires a sales call? Typically, if your chosen price is above $995 then you will struggle to sell it via a written sales page because it's hard to build up the level of trust required for someone to send you a larger amount than this without speaking to a human first. Within my e-learning company we have tested many different prices – from $495 to $1,995 and everywhere in between – and I can tell you with absolute certainty that one performs head and shoulders above the rest: that price is $995.

I absolutely guarantee that if you have an engaged email list of over 2,500 people and you send them a re-offer, as long as your written sales page is written properly, you will make money. I have run re-offers for many years, and every single one of my business coaching clients have sent at least one – providing they had the ability to do so – and I have never seen less than $23,000 in sales, depending on the amount of leads within the database, of course.

This section of the book alone will make you a 100,000 per cent return on the price you paid for this book.

The following is the main re-offer email we use, and have used for the last two years – yes, we reuse the same email every time, and run a re-offer every six months.

Once you've decided when to send your re-offer, take the following email and rewrite the subject line and the introductory body copy, just like I did with the previous emails I shared. Don't worry, I'll give you some examples of subject lines and lead-ins after we've covered the email itself.

Subject line:

[first name], you've been selected

Body copy:

[First Name],

If you're receiving this email, you've been selected to get access to the brand new June 2023 version of our Platinum Program. Which is our flagship trading program, where you learn our unique, mechanical trading strategies, that provide a statistical edge over the markets.

Allowing you to trade profitably by just following a simple set of mechanical "rules". Over the last few months, I've rebuilt our flagship program, and we're almost ready to release it publicly.

Before that happens though, *we're looking for just 25 people to "test-drive" the new program content.* And in return for your time and feedback, we're letting you in with a $5,205 discount.

That means *forget the usual $6,800 price-tag.* You won't pay that. You'll be able to get full access for just $995 instead. *But* this is only for the first 25 people who go to this page and who join now, today. (The 25 spots will be gone in a few hours).

Seriously, if you're in now, you save $5,805. If you miss this though, it's off the table. Gone, finito. No exceptions. Click here to download the mechanical rules now. So [first name], if you are still going through the pain of pouring your hard-earned dough down the drain in losses to the markets. If you are still stuck in the rat-race, on the hamster wheel, in need of a way to begin pulling money out of the markets now. If you are lacking a strategy, a framework, an edge over the market along with simple, clear rules to follow. Wondering if you'll ever finally learn to trade profitably.

Click here to access the full program immediately [insert a link]

And let's finally turn your trading around together

You'll have access to everything that we offer:

– All four of our key strategies, worth $2,380

– A personal success manager assigned to you, worth $995

– Our 'trader development' resources, worth $147

– 3 x complimentary one-to-one coaching sessions, worth $197 each

- A 'secret' once per week 'edge' that offers a regular +2R win, worth $995

- An entire year of group coaching calls with all other Platinum clients, worth $1,925

That's a genuine total value of $7,033. But by joining today, you'll get it all for $995.

But I have to stress this: As soon as the 25 spots are taken, the doors are closed for good. Again, no exceptions. I hope the above helps [first name], and we look forward to sharing the brand new version of the Platinum Program with you.

- To your success

Will

p.s. Want to see the kind of results our clients have achieved using the mechanical rules you're about to learn inside the Platinum Program? If so, here they are for you [insert a link]

That email has made me hundreds of thousands of dollars. In fact, almost a million dollars now, to be exact. It will do the same for you when it is reworded to suit your niche and offer, as you send it out every six months over the coming years to your leads.

Next, duplicate this email five times – you'll send your re-offer out at five specific times of the day, 9am, 1pm, 5pm, 9pm and 11pm – and create four other subject lines and email lead-ins.

Here are a few of my highest-performing subject lines:

- You OK?
- Re: Final Notice
- Re: Can't see your name on the list?
- [First Name] is about to lose out on $5,805
- [First Name] your [insert the name of your program] login

Use those as inspiration, and obviously tailor the introduction to each email – the first few lines, or so – to match the subject line to aid congruence. If you do not do this, people will experience sales resistance and will unsubscribe.

The key to increasing funnel efficiency

Earlier in the book, I explained how to build a sales funnel, but setting one up isn't enough – you also need to optimise it. If you do not track your sales funnel numbers, you're not going to succeed. Full stop. You cannot run a successful, profitable business, let alone a sales funnel, without knowing your numbers. This is one of the number one problems that prevents success.

I have a tracking spreadsheet to track the most important numbers in my sales funnel – everything from ad spend and impressions to opt-in page conversion and booked calls, and plenty more. The template I use came from Sam Ovens and was shared with me when I joined his Quantum mastermind. It is a phenomenal tool for revealing the bottlenecks in sales funnels and, therefore, showing you exactly what needs to be fixed.

You can download the template by visiting:

www.howtotenmillion.com/resources

These are the average metrics of a successful, profitable business (all of which are tracked on the spreadsheet):

- CPM – cost per thousand impressions: $15
- CTR – click-through rate: 1%
- LP% – landing page conversion rate: 20%
- CPL – cost per-lead: $10
- VCR% – video conversion rate: 10%
- SHOW – show-up rate: 55%
- TAKEN – taken call cost: $250
- CLOSE – close rate: 25%
- CPA – cost per acquisition: $1,000

The closer you can get to those numbers, the better. If you can land on them, then congratulations, you now have a money-printing machine. If you can beat them, then even better. Mathematically speaking, if you can make a sale for a $1,000 cost per acquisition, as in the above case, and the price of your program is $2,000 or anywhere above this, then you now have the ability to double your money, or greater, on demand.

As a caveat, the above metrics will change depending on two things:

1. The quality of your sales funnel.
2. Your offer and price point.

Diagnosing a broken funnel

The easiest way to spot which part of your funnel is broken – or underperforming – is to look for low numbers. It sounds simple, and it really is. So, if you have an offer that no-one wants, you will see a low CTR because no one is clicking on your ad. If this is the case, all the numbers in your funnel will likely be low – and you'll be making very few sales.

If your offer is fantastic and you're getting a lot of clicks on your ads, to diagnose any issue further into your funnel look for the first point at which the numbers drop and start there, as this is your bottleneck.

Often it doesn't take much to fix a bottleneck once you know it's there. For example, one of my business coaching clients came to me with a landing page conversion percentage of just 5.8 per cent, which is extremely low given the average is 20 per cent. This was preventing the traffic from flowing through the rest of his funnel, meaning he had almost no leads, almost no sales calls, and almost no sales.

We fixed this by doing two things:

1. We rewrote his headline – which is the most important aspect of the whole page.
2. We added three video testimonials at the bottom to increase trust.

This instantly brought his opt-in percentage up to 17.4 per cent and made the funnel highly profitable.

As another example, one of my business coaching clients came to me as he could not close sales calls. His sales script was, well, complete and utter rubbish. He was not removing objections, he was breaking rapport, he was not holding prospects accountable, there was no financial qualification during the calls, and his close rate was a terrible seven per cent.

We fixed this by rewriting his script and role-playing it together until it felt completely natural, and he felt able to handle objections if they occurred. Within a month, he was closing at 21 per cent which, whilst not a breathtaking close rate, was more than enough to make the funnel highly profitable.

All bottlenecks can be fixed, so never worry if you experience one. Use the sheet to identify them, then use the knowledge you learn from this book to fix them, and you'll do extremely well.

Tips for fixing broken funnel components

Next, let's discuss how to fix broken or low-performing funnel components, starting with your ads and, more specifically, your click-through-rate.

If you're seeing a low click-through rate, which I define as 0.4 per cent or lower, your ads are not good enough. This could mean the hook or the general copy is not strong enough, you're putting people off in the ad itself, the visual aspects are not stimulating enough, or the audio quality is letting the ad down. The bottom line is you need to create new ads.

I always suggest that my clients start with at least 20 ads and run these for seven days without touching them, to let the advertising platform's algorithm optimise the ads. In regards to budget, $10 per ad is solid to begin with, equaling $50 per day ad spend and $350 for the seven-day period in total.

To create 20 ads, write two full ad scripts and five hooks. Then, attach one hook onto each of the two full ad scripts. This will create 10 ads that are ready for production. From there, I suggest making 10 PowerPoint and voiceover versions, and 10 in-person versions. Voila, you now have 20 ads to test with.

From there, you should have at least one ad that performs at a solid rate, which I define as 0.8 per cent or higher. If you do not see an ad performing at this level, then you must start again by creating five more ads and repeating this process.

If you do, then take the ad or ads that perform, turn off the others and roll the $50 per day budget into the ads that have shown promise. From there, create five new hooks – the first five to ten seconds of the ad – and edit these onto the body of the best-performing ad. Launch these five new ads at $10 per ad and repeat the process one more time.

The goal here is to get at least two or three ads with a click-through rate of at least 0.8 per cent. When you have this, you are all set and you can leave these ads to run for months. Please note, I am specifically focusing on YouTube as an advertising platform here, as it's the cheapest and most highly-targeted ad platform currently available.

Dropping knowledge: a guide to CTR performance

0.4 per cent CTR or below – Your ad is not good enough.

0.4 to 0.8 per cent CTR – Your ad is good, but is not great.

0.8 to 1.2 per cent CTR – Your ad is fantastic, very well done.

1.2 per cent CTR or higher - Wow. Awesome work!

After you have two or three high-performing ads under your belt, it's time to focus on the next step of the funnel, your opt-in page, where your primary aim is to collect a prospect's contact details in exchange for free training or a lead magnet.

A good opt-in rate is 20 per cent. If you know your audience well, it's likely you'll be able to write a great opt-in almost immediately. If you do not fully and intimately know your audience, it might take you a few tries to nail a great opt-in page, but don't give up. You'll get there. Keep playing with the headline, the sub-headline, the image and the info bullet points until you land on a solid opt-in rate.

Dropping knowledge: a guide to opt-in rate performance

10 per cent or below opt-in rate – Cause for concern, your opt-in is not good enough.

10 to 15 per cent opt-in rate – Good job, this is not great, but it'll certainly do.

15 to 20 per cent opt-in rate – You've nailed it. You clearly know your stuff.

20 per cent or higher opt-in rate – You've bought my business coaching program, haven't you?

If you're struggling with your opt-in, keep in mind that 70 per cent of its performance is in the big, bold headline at the top. The pre-headline and the headline itself are crucial. Here are a few questions and things I keep in mind when writing a headline for one of my clients:

- What do your audience want to avoid at all costs?
- What do your audience desire most deeply?
- What do your audience not only hate, but also despise?
- What keeps your audience up at night, tossing and turning?
- What do your audience fear the most? What chills them to their very bones?

- What kind of promise will make opting in for your free training a no-brainer?
- What kind of promise will remain believable so it doesn't raise any scepticism?
- What big juicy steak of a promise would your audience leap at submitting their info to watch?
- What are your audience starving for, what would they do anything to gain, or to achieve?

You get the gist. Sell them what they want, without any of the things they hate.

Be big and bold, but believable. If they're made sceptical, they'll bounce from the page.

When you've answered the above questions and you have built a great opt-in page, you'll be generating a metric tonne of leads, and you'll have hundreds of people headed towards the next step in your funnel, which will either be a VSL or a webinar, depending on which you've decided to build.

Either way, what we're now focused on is the percentage of viewers who book a call. Typically, if your video is solid, you'll see around a ten per cent view-to-booking rate. If you're below five per cent, your video is simply not good enough. If you're above 15 per cent, you've absolutely nailed it, well done.

If you follow the VSL training I provided earlier in this book, there's a very high chance you'll create a great sales video on your first attempt. If you struggle, however, one option may be to hire a copywriter or even join my business coaching so I can help you. Another would be to read some copywriting books and brush up on the skill for yourself and create new versions until you're converting viewers to bookings at a good enough rate.

From experience, most of my business coaching clients nail their sales video on their first attempt, but don't worry if it takes you two or three rebuilds. None of us are copywriting experts immediately.

When you've created a sales video that converts, you'll have calls flooding in like a torrential downpour. The next step in the funnel is having these prospects show up. In most cases, by simply enabling some SMS and email reminders inside your call booking application – I use Calendly – your show rate will be good from the off.

Dropping knowledge: a guide to show rate performance

35 per cent show rate or below – Something's very wrong. Are your reminders enabled?

35 to 45 per cent – This is not great, but it's doable if your lead cost is on the low side.

45 to 55 per cent – This is industry standard, but it could be better.

55 per cent or above – Wow. Fantastic. You're doing something very right.

As I explained earlier, our average show rate for almost three years sat at between 50 and 55 per cent. This is solid, but it could be better. Over the last month, me and my team have focused on raising this and have got it up to 67 per cent by enabling an instant SMS message that confirms the booking when it's made, along with sending a 20-second personalised Loom video via Whatsapp, or email if the prospect does not have Whatsapp.

This increase has changed the game for our sales team.

Here's our Loom script so you can swipe it:

"Hey [first name], it's just Adam from WBTrading. I can see you've booked in with me for tomorrow at 1pm, super excited for our call. You've made a great decision by booking in. Any questions before then, just write them down and we'll cover them on the call. See you tomorrow Adam."

Easy as that. If you follow all of this advice, you'll most likely have a show rate of 60 per cent or above and you're all set to close your first few clients and add a few thousand dollars to your soon-to-be-bulging bank balance. The final thing to optimise is your sales skills and ability – and I covered how to optimise your sales script in Chapter 7, so revisit this if this is your bottleneck.

SMS: the highest ROI lever you can pull

I only discovered the power of SMS around a year ago through an automation expert called Lisa Catto, who asked if I wanted to have the ability to send SMS added to our CRM system. I told her I'd never thought about it, and she proceeded to tell me that the average open rate of an SMS is a staggering 90 per cent plus, compared to only 35 per cent for email. We tried it, sending a very short, sharp nine-word-style message to our database of leads who had not yet bought from us, and booked sales calls for as low as $7 per call.

SMS changed my e-learning company completely due to its low cost of booking sales calls with existing leads. It seems like common sense, doesn't it? If you have people's phone numbers, why not send them an SMS leading them to book a call?

Do not ignore this piece of guidance. If you are not collecting phone numbers on your opt-in page, start doing so immediately. If you are collecting phone numbers, but you are not using SMS, again, do so immediately. Do not leave money on the table like we did. All you need to do is draft a quick message that is to-the-point, add a link to your calendar, and hit send. Depending on how many leads are in your database, you'll quickly book a handful of calls, and at a very low cost. Currently, it costs us $25 to send 250 SMS messages, which usually books us around four to six calls.

To help you get started, here's our standard SMS script:

"Hey [first name] it's Will from WBTrading. How's your trading going? Do you still need help? If yes, here's my calendar so you can book in a strategy-session call with me: [link] Speak soon – Will".

It's as easy as that.

The value of "setting" sales calls

What is "setting" I hear you ask? It's the act of phoning your leads for a quick five to ten minute call to "set" them up for a sales call.

This technique dramatically increases the profitability of a sales funnel by making sure that every lead possible books a call. After all, we all know that life can get in the way sometimes. It's not uncommon for leads to get distracted after opting into a funnel, or whilst watching the sales video, thus forgetting to proceed to booking in a call.

You can employ a "setter" – a specific member of your team whose job is to make these calls – or you can do them yourself. Either way, the aim is to maximise the number of sales calls that are booked, rather than letting some fall through the cracks.

I suggest using Close.io in order to call your leads, which is sales CRM software that stores all of your leads and allows you to call them from within the app at a very low rate of, at the time of writing, around $0.08 per minute, depending on the country you're calling. Alternatively, the Yolla app for iPhone also works well, allowing for international calls at an extremely low rate of around $0.06 per minute, depending on the country you're calling. We used both within my e-learning company.

Here's a walk-through of my setting script from my e-learning company. Be sure to reword the questions to suit your niche and offer after you've understood the script and the concept.

"Hey, is this [first name]?

Hey [first name], it's just Will from WBTrading, I'm calling about the mechanical trading rules video you signed up to watch earlier. I just wanted to make sure you were able to access it OK because we've had a technical glitch with it today. Were you able to view it?"

Here, we're using very specific wording, for example it's "just" Will calling, which makes them feel like we might have spoken before, or that they know me and I am not a threat or a cold caller. It softens the interaction and makes them more likely to open up. "We had a technical glitch with it" is our excuse for calling, which again, reduces sales resistance and opens them up to the conversation.

"Ah, perfect. And I'm not sure if you read this on the page, but you were also supposed to get a more in-depth, more specific training on how mechanical rules are actually built from one of William's paid programs. Has anyone reached out about that yet?"

This is a little sneaky because it doesn't exist, so obviously no-one has reached out about it. The reason we say this is to justify asking them questions in order to qualify them. Naturally, we can't say to them; "Hey, I'm just calling to qualify you for a sales call so I can sell you my program." We have to instead be covert.

"OK, well the reason you didn't get it immediately is just 'cause we have two different training videos and we wanted to make sure you got something that was actually relevant to what you're struggling with within your trading at the moment. Is that something I can get to you? Great to hear, let's do it. And just so that I know which one of the two trainings to send you, would you mind if I ask two super-quick questions so I know which one of the two will be better for you?"

Here, we've justified why we need to ask them questions. The door is now open for us to qualify them.

"Awesome, so, how long have you been trading for now? I see, and if you had to name one single thing that's holding your trading back, what would you say that would be?

Understood, and is this whole trading thing more of a side-hustle kind of thing or is this a more serious pursuit where you'd like to make it a career in the long-term? Got it, and just so I can get a feel for where you're at, how much capital are you trading with at the moment?

If they say "why are you asking" then you'd say: Sure, no worries, so the only reason I ask that is because obviously working with us isn't free, and if we do find that you're a good fit for the program, we want you to see a return on investment as soon as possible, and obviously the more capital you're trading with, the sooner that happens, so that's the only reason I ask.

If they are not qualified: OK, got it. Perfect, well I know exactly which of the two trainings to send you so I'll get that over for you in a sec. That aside, enjoy the training and best of luck with everything!

If they are qualified: OK, got it. Perfect, well I know exactly which of the two trainings to send you so I'll get that over for you in a sec, and in fact, based on what you've told me there, I think you might benefit from a strategy session call with one of our lead advisors here at WBTrading, so that they can walk you through how our mechanical rules work, to see if they'd help you with your own trading. Would you be up for that?

Great to hear, well let's book it in for you. When would be best for you, Tuesday or Wednesday this week? Great, and what time would work best for you? Perfect, right, I'll get that booked in for you, and just to check, will you 100 per cent be able to make that time or is there any chance you might have to reschedule? No worries at all, perfect stuff.

Right, so that's all booked in for you [first name], so I'll get that free training video over for you right now via email, if you have any thoughts or questions in the meantime write them down and you can cover those on the call with William when you sit down with him. Have a great rest of the day!"

Voilà. You've just set a qualified sales call. One final tip to share with you in regards to setting – the sooner that you dial the lead after they opt in, the more sets you'll be able to book. Think about it, if you opted in five days ago, you've likely forgotten all about the ad you clicked or the opt-in you saw, whereas if you just opted in five minutes ago, it's fresh in your mind and you're still in the pain or problem state that made you click the ad to land on the opt-in page in the first place.

Action points

If you don't already have a means of tracking the performance of each component of your funnel, I recommend you download the template I've shared and start doing exactly this. It's only when you can see where the problem is that you can find the most appropriate way to fix it. I'm not kidding when I say knowing the numbers around your funnel's performance is the difference between making tens of thousands and hundreds of thousands of dollars.

Chapter 11

Tactics for Scaling

Scaling is just another way of saying growing in the business world. The simplest formula for scaling is customer lifetime value (LTV) over cost per acquisition (CPA). Put in the simplest terms, you need to make sure that your customer spends more with you than whatever it costs you to make a sale.

Scaling a business really is that simple. It's nothing more than mathematics.

Calculating LTV and CPA

To work out the LTV of your customers, all you need to know is how much your customers spend with you across a six to 12-month period. Bear in mind your front-end program, your back-end program(s), if any, and any additional services they

buy, such as one-off coaching or perhaps a software subscription. Your LTV is the average your customers spend.

You calculate your CPA by dividing your monthly ad spend by the number of customers you bring in each month. If you want to scale, then your LTV should be a *minimum* of 1.5x to 2x your CPA. So, if it costs you $500 to make a sale, you should be capturing a minimum of $750 in LTV from each sale, equaling a 1.5x return. If your return is lower than this, it is likely to dip to break-even or a loss as you scale, due to rising advertising costs.

In an ideal world, you'll be spending around $500 to $1,000 to acquire a sale of $2,000 plus.

To bring this into the real world, within my e-learning company it was costing us roughly $950 to make an $8,500 front-end program sale through paid advertising, and each customer's LTV was around the $10,000 mark (over six to 12 months) considering our $7,000 mastermind and our $350 per-month recurring software on the back-end of the business.

I also see these numbers, or similar ones, within other businesses I work with. On average, as long as the offer and the funnel are strong, it costs around $1,000 to $1,500 to make a sale. Imagine if you could run paid ads and make a sale at that cost. As long as the price of your program is anything above those numbers, then congratulations, you now own a money-printing machine.

Dropping knowledge: what does a good funnel generate?

If you've just started running paid ads to a new funnel, with a new offer at a high-ticket price point, at low-scale – for example spending $100 to $250 per day – then you should be seeing 3–4x cash returns and 5–6x revenue returns at the start. This is the sign of a healthy funnel.

As you scale, and as I mentioned earlier in this book, naturally these numbers will slowly reduce due to advertising platforms charging more as you spend more. You will combat this by writing new ads, training better sales reps, raising the price of your program, introducing back-end products and services, introducing up-sells or down-sells, and so on, to bolster each customer's LTV.

To scale, you'll need to make more upfront "day one" cash than it costs you to acquire sales or you'll fall into the red. Some companies scale into the red knowing that their lifetime value will still leave them profitable, but it's a dangerous game to play. I don't encourage it.

How to reduce CPA

Firstly, *make newer, better ads* that are specifically written to "sell the click". Remember, the only job of an ad is to grab your avatar, wow them and get them to click the ad. Your only focus when writing an ad should be to sell the click.

Secondly, *make a new, better opt-in page* that "sells the mechanism". Remember, the only job of the opt-in page is to intrigue your avatar, wow them and get them to submit their contact details to get more information on what your unique mechanism is. That is the sole purpose of your headline, and everything else on the page.

Thirdly, *consider making a new, more compelling VSL* that "sells the call" and portrays the value of booking a call with you, or that gets them so excited about the "secret" or your "method" that they feel compelled to book a call with you.

Another way to reduce CPA is to train your sales team to close at a higher rate. This will raise your cash collected and enable you to bring down your CPA very quickly. You can achieve this through roleplay sessions with your team, as well as objection handling classes, making sure they fully understand the sales script and why they're saying what they're saying. I also encourage purchasing outside education for them – whether that's a course, a coaching program, or a mastermind. You're looking for anything you can do for them to make them better.

Fourthly, *consider introducing a complete no-brainer, action-based guarantee,* whereby if your client does not get the intended result, you'll simply refund them with no questions asked. This removes the risk of purchasing and, as long as they believe and trust you, makes buying a genuine no-brainer. Be careful with this though, because if it sounds "too good to be true" it will raise scepticism and act against you.

One way of removing this scepticism is through a written contract, and making this clear on your sales page. Wording like: "It is legally contracted inside our program, and we, therefore, have to honour the guarantee, so long as you meet the criteria" will work. You'll set the criteria of the guarantee based on what the client must do in order to achieve success. For example, they might need to watch all of the course content, attend at least four coaching calls, and use the [knowledge they'll learn] and put it into tangible action. Make it clear that, if they do those three things and do not achieve the [promised result] in three months, then they qualify for your guarantee.

Lastly, *improve your offer*. Make sure it's simple, easy, fast, push-button, without the things people hate and within one of the three pillars of pain I shared in Chapter 2. Tick those boxes and you'll have a very low CPA.

As an example, the offer behind my e-learning company at WBTrading was: "Follow a set of rules, learn them in 15 minutes, and you'll then consistently make money, with certainty and predictability, without hours sat staring at the charts and without any of the complex analysis that's held you back so far."

In other words: It's easy, it's fast, you'll get exactly what you want instantly, with certainty, and without any of the stuff that's held you back so far. We have a very unique mechanism – mechanical rules. Before we started scaling into the market, no-one knew what this was, and to this day my sales team get people on calls who say they've never heard of this method of trading, so this offer was – and still is – incredibly strong. That, plus the results we achieved for our clients allowed us to build a great business and scale far.

How to increase LTV

Firstly, *raise the price of your program*. Low pricing is often based on the insecurities of the founder. If you're wondering if you really can charge a high price for your offer, don't worry, it's natural. After all, I first sold my offer for $50 back when I first launched my Word document!

Simply raising your price works incredibly well. I did this many, many times in my e-learning company and every single time it raised our cash collected. In my own experience, I've never seen this not be effective, both for my business, my friends' businesses and every single business coaching client I've ever worked with.

Secondly, *introduce a back-end product or service*. This could be in-person coaching via video, a retreat, a mastermind, a down-sell product, a book – there are lots of things you can "bolt-on" to raise lifetime value. Get creative and have fun with this. One of my business coaching clients is currently offering one full day at his home in Dubai with him for $10,000 as an up-sell for his existing customers. He sold five of these one-day sessions when he launched the offer. We created the offer a week prior, whilst brainstorming ways to add additional value for his clients.

What up-sell can you create right now that will add value for your clients? Think it up, and launch it to your customers by emailing them, and just watch your bank balance explode to the upside.

Aside from up-sells, you can also down-sell your leads – the people who have not yet bought from you – into a "lite" version of your program as just one idea, as I explained in Chapter 5.

Another useful technique can be only offering your program for a set time period and then charging to keep access to the

content – for example, $5,000 to join, and then $250 per month to keep access. Again, play with this and have fun with it. There are no rules or restrictions here. What pricing structure satisfies you, and also works for your clients? What pricing structure allows you to scale as far as you want to? The great thing about this specific model of charging an entry fee and then a recurring fee is that it compounds on itself as you scale.

Keep in mind all of the above tips and techniques when it comes to reducing CPA and also increasing customer LTV, and use these levers to adjust the output of the machine that is your education and coaching business.

Pipeline, follow-up and nurture

As simple as it sounds, if you've had a call with someone who does not close there and then, do not ignore them after the call ends. I suggest keeping detailed notes on every person you speak to, and following up with them on a schedule. Keep it simple. Follow up after a week, after three weeks, after six weeks and after nine weeks. You'll be surprised how many additional deals you close by doing this.

In fact, recently I prompted one of my clients to do this after I noticed that he'd taken some quality calls over the last couple of weeks that hadn't closed. These were people that should certainly have invested in his program. By taking my advice and using his detailed notes for reference, he was able to close a $3,000 sale that he otherwise would not have captured.

When it comes to following up and nurturing your prospects, there are two main ways I've found to be most effective:

1. Following up with value by sending them one of your new YouTube videos, blog posts, X post streams, or similar. It simply needs to be something helpful that they'll benefit from.
2. Reminding them of your conversation by referencing your detailed notes, and asking where they are in relation to solving their problem. If they still have not solved their problem, use this as a way to arrange a follow-up call with them. On the follow-up, reiterate your pitch

and attempt to close them. If they push back, affirm to them that surely if they could have solved their problem alone, they would have done so by now. Use their lack of success to make it clear that they do need help, and position yourself as the trusted authority who can make that a reality.

Automation

Automation of tasks – be those business, or even personal tasks – will make your life easier, reduce stress and increase scale. But automation must be used properly – go overboard and you'll destroy your business. I should know, I've made this mistake myself.

In year three of my business, I used an automated "fake-live" webinar to make sales. I would run paid ads to plug the webinar, people would register to watch it, and then all-hell would ensue in regards to automation. Complex email contingencies would begin firing based on the day someone registered, the viewing time they selected and how much of the webinar they watched, if any. Replay sequences would race away in the background. Offer emails would burst into action based on whether they watched some, or all, of the webinar. It was a maze of complexity.

My thinking was that it would help to make sure that people would be able to watch the webinar, rewatch it if they missed it, be reminded of the replay, be reminded of the offer and so on. It actually felt great building it, but in the end, it trapped me inside the web I'd created; like a fly trapped in a spider's lair.

Automations ended up breaking, and it would take us days to realise, meaning we lost many sales. Email contingencies ended up breaking, meaning new leads would receive discount codes not due to be given to them until weeks later. It was a mess.

Don't make this silly mistake. Keep your sales funnel dead simple. It's more beneficial for both you and your prospects. I've already told you all you need to run a successful sales funnel, as well as shared a few basic email contingencies that fire as people get stuck. Use all of this knowledge to your advantage.

Automation should help you, not hinder you.

So, what should you automate, or outsource where automation isn't possible?

Six fundamentals to automate or outsource

1. **Emails:** as already suggested. You can do this inside Keap which is the best email software in the world, but is costly, or inside ActiveCampaign which is just as great, but a little bit less powerful, yet much cheaper.
2. **Vetting your sales call bookings**: you can do this using Typeform to set cancellation actions for people who

submit certain answers. This means for any demographic you know won't be likely to buy (as you've discovered using survey mathematics), they will have their call automatically cancelled and will be sent to a page featuring a video explaining why. Alternatively, you can hire a VA to manually cancel low-quality calls for you, which is my preference.

3. **Coaching, as you scale:** at a certain point, you might begin to hate being tied to coaching calls. You can outsource this by hiring a coach. I suggest hiring one of your best customers, which is what I did. Then, simply let them handle coaching calls for you.

4. **Customer support:** I used to love this, but similar to coaching, grew to hate it due to its never-ending demand on my time and energy. You can solve this by, again, hiring one of your best customers to take over this role.

5. **Running your ads, or even managing your sales team:** in my e-learning company, we outsourced the running of our ads to a great company called AdLeg for a monthly fee. On the sales side of things, there are many great companies that do everything from hiring and training sales reps, to coaching them and even managing the team for you. I strongly suggest this, as building your own sales team, especially as you scale up to five-plus reps, is a huge undertaking.

6. **Financial tasks such as bookkeeping and accounting:** I strongly suggest this as your very first hire as it is critical, as we discussed earlier, to know and to stay on top of your numbers. Hire a bookkeeper, and

make sure they are great at what they do. I'd encourage you to over-pay for the best financial control staff that you can find as it's a very important part of a business.

There are a couple of things I've left out, such as hiring a copywriter or someone to take over your social media account management and content creation, but those are helpful extras. What I've shared above are the six fundamental things that you should automate or outsource first, in no particular order, aside from bookkeeping which I suggest as the first thing you hire for as you scale.

Hiring the team you need

Want to seriously scale to some large numbers? You'll need to bring in some help.

When the time is right and you're pulling in serious moolah – I'm talking $100,000 to $250,000 per month in sales revenue or above – it's time to hire a copywriter to take over writing your email and sales copy. It's also time to hire someone to start producing your ads and perhaps even social media content for you, and you might even want to bring in a CEO or someone to manage the business for you, too. Having all of these people in place will allow you to solely focus on those top one per cent tasks that fuel huge growth – such as creating the vision for the company's future, building up your culture, conducting key meetings, thinking about product concepts or marketing strategies and so on.

This is the stage where you begin to remove yourself from everything, but the highest-level tasks.

Action points

I hope that, by now, you're realising just how much money is often left on the table by business owners who are unaware of the tips, tactics and strategies I'm sharing with you in this book. Use all of this knowledge to your advantage, take action and implement everything you've learned – it will give you a huge edge. You will make a lot of money, and will add a lot of value to the world, by doing so.

Before you move on, calculate your current customer LTV and CPA. Then see if there are any tactics I've shared that you can implement to nudge one or both of these higher.

Chapter 12

Vision, Team and Culture

What is your vision for your company?

Are you building a lifestyle business that makes you a little $10,000 to $30,000 a month so that you can travel the world and enjoy life, or a cash flow business that makes you $50,000 to $250,000 per month so that you can buy your dream house, car and invest in real estate to rapidly build wealth? Or are you building a corporation that makes you $500,000 to $1,000,000 or more per month so that you can have a huge impact on the world, develop amazing products and services, have offices all over the world and provide jobs for others? Or perhaps your passion is business, income is irrelevant and you're building for no other reason than fun and fulfilment? Or maybe you're building a business in order to exit one day?

Sometimes you'll start with one, and end with another. Whichever one you choose – big or small, lots of staff or zero staff, office or no office – using what you learn in this book, and with some hard work, over time you will achieve it. You will succeed and make all of the money you desire and deserve.

My business was initially created to generate cash flow. Nothing more. Put crudely, I started my e-learning company in order to make myself rich so that I could buy real estate with cash, generate a passive $10,000 per month, turn the business off and retire to go and pursue whatever I found fun.

Seven years later, and I had achieved exactly that, with one exception – I exited rather than turning the business off. That was all thanks to a mentor of mine, Dan Bradbury, who taught me how to make my business saleable. I didn't know a thing about selling a business, and I didn't believe, at the time, that it was possible for me. If it wasn't for being a part of Dan's mastermind, I would not have built my business so that it was saleable, and I would have missed out on a multi-million dollar payday when I sold my business to a private equity firm who own and operate it to this day.

Although my business started out as a "cash flow" business, due to how fast it grew it morphed into a "small corporation" with a team of 16 employees – all working remotely – making $800,000+ per-month in sales revenue. Then thanks to Dan's help and mentoring, it grew into a company I was able to exit.

My point is, your business can start out with one purpose and morph into having another purpose later. But, if you do want to exit one day, you have to build it in a way that allows that. You have to be entirely, or almost entirely, removed from operations. You have to have a solid financial track record of growth and profitability, with solid, well-kept financial documentation via a good bookkeeper and accountant. You have to have a great product, product-market fit and must take good care of your customers, and so on.

If you simply want a little cash flow business, however, you need none of that. Frankly, you don't even need a particularly ground-breaking product or service. You just need to make a good offer, build a good sales funnel and be good at sales. Of course, I am not suggesting you sell a rubbish product, that would be unethical. My point is that even if your initial product is sub-par, you can still quite easily make $10,000 to $30,000 per month due to nothing more than unit economics – as long as you are good at sales and you can close people on the phone.

Why am I telling you all of this? Because if you want to scale, you need to have a clear plan and a future vision in order to do so. You need to know where you're headed. As the saying goes: *"If you fail to plan, then you are planning to fail."* Without a plan, you're in a car driving without an end destination – and that means you won't know where or when to stop. However, if you understand where that end destination is for you, and precisely what it looks like, then you'll get there.

What is your vision?

Be honest with yourself. Your life is yours to create and enjoy, so go wild. Why not achieve everything you've ever dreamed of? Life is too short not to, and using what you learn in this book, you will have the skills and knowledge to achieve anything you want. Again though, speaking from experience, I encourage you to not only dream big, but to understand that there's more to life than just money. Sure, earn money and become a millionaire, but then pursue your passions, chase fun and fulfilment, and build great things.

This is the reason that I spend my time doing business coaching. It is my absolute passion, I love building businesses and helping people do the same. Writing this book is an absolute joy, I have loved the experience of writing it and, as I type this, right now, I hope that it allows you to make all the money you want and to get everything you've ever dreamed of. This to me is so incredibly fun.

Here are a few questions to ask yourself to help you craft your vision:

- If I owned all of the material things I ever wanted, what would I then do with my days?
- If I knew I could not fail, what would I choose to spend my time building or creating?
- What would I do with my days if money was no object?
- What impact do I want to have on the world?
- What fulfils me, and what do I love to do?
- How do I want to be remembered?

Anything is possible, so dream big!

Hire slow, fire fast

Once you have established your vision and decided on the type of business you want to build, you will likely discover you need to hire a team. Hiring, and the people you have within your business, will either make it or break it – it's no exaggeration to say hiring properly is crucial.

If you hire badly, the people will frustrate your customers, damage your product, cause harm to your reputation and more

– not to mention costing you a lot of time, headaches, stress and money. If you hire well, the people will make your customers happier, will help to improve your product, will improve your reputation and more – not to mention saving you time, reducing stress and making you a lot more money.

I first realised the true importance of a wider team when I was taught about the depth of the president of the United States' team. Of course I didn't think he made every all-important decision on his own, but understanding that he had a board of advisors, various different cabinets filled with key decision makers, various different consultants and internal report staff and so on made me respect just how many layers there are to how decisions are reached, and how the overall presidential enterprise functions. It's no different from running a business. In order to build and grow a successful, formidable company, you need those same layers for yourself, to aid in accurate decision-making.

The phrase "hire slow, fire fast" is a simple and accurate one, but it's often ignored. Please, take heed. You must hire slowly – interview someone once yourself, then have another trusted team member interview again, check their references, and so on – and fire fast. If someone makes serious mistakes, fire them. I've learned this the hard way – a leopard doesn't change its spots. If you ever "feel" like firing someone, that is your warning sign. Don't ignore it, or it will cost you.

How do you hire?

There are several ways to hire from a logistical standpoint – you can email your customers, post in mastermind groups or use Indeed.com – but how do you hire from a qualitative, human standpoint? As I mentioned above, interview twice or more. Some of the greatest companies in the world – Goldman Sachs, for example – require over ten interviews, with ten different people. Yes, *over* ten interviews in order to receive a job offer. Why? Because they know how much a bad hire costs them from a time, energy and money standpoint. As a result, they take hiring deadly seriously.

You should, too.

Interviewing is step one. Experience is step two. Can you speak to a reference? Do they have call recordings, tracking sheets, awards, or other evidence of their past performance, to prove that they can deliver on the role you're hiring for? From there, if you do choose to hire them, your month one impression of them is the final piece of the puzzle. Do they onboard well, do they get on with the rest of the team, do they contribute, are they on time for meetings, and so on? What does your gut tell you about them?

If you feel you've made a mistake, let go of them quickly. Don't worry, you'll master hiring – and firing – given time and experience. For most people, it is a pain, but it's one that's necessary in order to grow your business, make you money, and serve your clients and customers at the highest level possible.

Culture and values

I used to hate the word "culture" – I always thought of it as boring business lingo. *I don't need culture, I need sales* or *let's just hire talented people and leave them to work*, were some of my thoughts and beliefs when it came to culture.

I soon learned that I was wrong when my first team member quit. They had asked me for a month off, which I do still feel is too heavy of a request. But nonetheless, I should have made it clear when I hired her that our culture within my company is one of focus and hard work, not taking a month off to travel Thailand, with three days' notice, no less. We were out of alignment from a culture standpoint, which was completely my own doing.

Learn from my mistakes ahead of hiring your first team member. Create your own culture based on your personal values, and make this clear when you hire people. Do you work seven days a week, or only four or five? Do you believe in "grinding" hard, or in flying by the seat of your pants and taking things as they come? Do you want to create a lifestyle business and only have a few clients join you per month, or a corporation that brings in 100+ clients per month?

Get clear on what you want your business to look and feel like. Know how fast you want to grow, how intense you want your level of focus to be, how many hours you are OK with working, and so on. Then, make sure that this culture is portrayed when hiring, so that you are in alignment with your team members, rather than out of alignment as I was when my first employee quit her job.

Similar to what I said above regarding what "your gut" tells you when you're onboarding a new team member, much of growing a business is not hard data, but instead, intuition. "Trust, but verify" is a saying that I love – or in other words, I'd say "use intuition, and then rest on data or past experience".

Here are a few questions to help you craft your culture:

- How many hours do I like to work per week?

- Do I like to "grind" hard, or take things as they come?
- Are entire weekends off something I want, or do I love working all the time?
- Am I focused on building a huge enterprise, or a cash flow and lifestyle-type business?

With those answered, and perhaps any other questions that come up for you out of the above also answered, collate what you've written down and build this into your own unique culture. When you hire people, make them aware of all aspects of your culture along with what you expect of them – be clear about the hours they'll work, the attitude you expect of them, their likely workload, the type of lifestyle you and them will lead by being a part of the business, and so on.

Next, let's discuss values. In fact, we kind of just have. What do you value? Time off, a huge income, freedom, working with people or remotely, wealth, giving to others, building incredible products or services, health and wellbeing? What makes you feel whole, fulfilled, and like you're growing and progressing?

In a way, this is why culture and values go together. I'd describe culture as what is expected, and values as what goes into what is expected. Culture is the cake, values are the ingredients that go into baking the cake.

By answering all of the above questions I've shared with you, you'll begin to understand your own "ingredients", and you'll

be able to begin creating and crafting your "cake" – in other words, your culture, which is unique to you and your business.

Action points

Take a look at the questions I've shared in this chapter and have a go at answering them to help you formulate your vision for your company and to help you better articulate what your company culture is. This will really help you when you start hiring, as it will improve your chances of finding right-fit team members.

Chapter 13

Capital Management

As your education company grows, you'll have more cash in the bank than you ever thought possible. I remember the first time I ever saw over $1,000,000 in my bank account. It was a joyous, but a worrying, moment. Why was it worrying? Because I was painfully aware that banks only insure up to $250,000 of the money you hold in a bank account, so if you have $1,000,000 and the bank goes bust, you've just lost three quarters of a million dollars irreversibly.

This is the real reason why entrepreneurs often invest in multiple expensive watches, a fleet of cars, multiple homes all over the world, multiple bank accounts in different countries and so on – not to show off, but to simply get their money out of the bank and de-risk it.

Jamie's story – the big freeze

To convey my point, I'd like to share my friend Jamie's painful story with you. Jamie started a business selling an online course on the subject of teaching medical doctors how to quit their job and begin a coaching business from home, teaching their subject remotely for a much larger income than they were being paid working within a practice. I didn't think much of the offer myself, but believe it or not, within a year Jamie was making in excess of $1,300,000 per month selling the offer globally.

Yep... Per month.

He was catapulted to an immense income faster than a bolt of lightning striking the earth – and an unexpected problem occurred. His bank froze his account pending an explanation of why, and how, he was making so much money. He was spending around $30,000 per day on ads and bringing in around $45,000 per day in sales revenue. These are very large amounts, and his bank flagged him as a result, requesting an in-person "know your customer" (or KYC) meeting. This is where a bank requests to see your passport, proof of address, business documents, customer information, and so on, to prove that you are who you say you are, and that your business – and income – are legitimate.

Suffice to say, Jamie willingly provided this, but with his bank account frozen for ten days, he had to turn off his ads and pause his business and his income. After he cleared up the mess and the bank approved his documents, he resumed business. But not for long.

Two months later, it happened again. The bank froze his account and asked for a second round of KYC proceedings. Let's just say Jamie was not pleased. After providing the necessary documents to his bank for a second time and again resuming business, he knew he had to do something to stop this happening again. So he decided to open up a secondary company in Dubai where he would run his Facebook ads, whilst using his existing business to run his YouTube ads, thus having two alternate bank accounts in order to spread his risk, and halving the advertising spend between each.

For the next four months, everything went smoothly. Until he received a call from his bank in Dubai, requesting an urgent KYC meeting. Worse still, their branch was located in another emirate, which required a three hour drive into the desert, twice across ten days. Jamie was now not only worried, but immensely stressed. "How am I being prevented from running a legitimate business, just because I make a lot of money and am successful? This is not fair, it's ridiculous!" he said.

It got worse.

The Dubai bank account was frozen for two long months, halving his business whilst it was addressed and eventually, unfrozen. Jamie quickly withdrew as much capital from the account as possible and stored it by buying a $1,700,000 apartment with cash, along with a Richard Mille watch for a further $400,000 in order to relieve some of the money from the bank – simply to regain some control over his own capital.

Note that he didn't make these large purchases to show off, he did so out of necessity. Whilst it was a highly stressful time in Jamie's life, needing to invest $2,000,000 in a piece of luxury real estate and a luxury timepiece is a nice problem to have, right?

I will pause the story of Jamie here by sharing that, in the end, by reducing his advertising spend and spreading it across three international bank accounts and business entities, he was able to safely resume operations, and he has never had a problem since.

Why did I share Jamie's story? Two reasons – the first is to paint the picture of just how much money you can make with one of these online education businesses, and how quickly. The second is to highlight how important managing, and more specifically investing, your money is. You must get it out of the bank and invest it into assets that you control.

Here are a few of my favourite investment vehicles.

Physical gold – This is easy to purchase, it can be stored in your home, you can also travel with it on your person, and it can be liquidated and turned back into cash quickly, wherever you are in the world.

Risk: medium.
Investment timeline: mid to long term.

Index funds – These are easy to purchase, are stored online so that you can access them from anywhere in the world, and they can be liquidated typically within three to five days and turned back into cash in the bank. They typically average a return of seven per cent per year and are one of the safest places to store, and grow, your money.

Risk: low.
Investment timeline: mid to long term.

Real estate – This can be difficult to purchase and, even if buying with cash, requires you to complete paperwork, often conduct meetings with an agent or a bank, and it can take months to finally own. Although it is illiquid – which means you cannot quickly get your money out – real estate is one of the safest assets in the world to invest in, returning, on average, six per cent per year. It's also a vehicle where you're able to store the largest amount of money. You can buy a $10,000,000 house if you want to get this amount of money out of the bank in one go.

Risk: low.
Investment timeline: mid to long term.

Watches – Similar to physical gold, watches are easy to purchase, can be stored in your home and you can also travel with them on your person. They can also be liquidated and turned back into cash quickly, wherever you are in the world. You can also store a large amount of money in one single watch – you could buy a $50,000 Rolex or a $150,000 Patek Phillippe, or a $500,000 Richard Mille. They can also be high-yielding investments, depending on what type of watch you buy, and when. As an example, I paid $32,000 for my Rolex President a year or so ago, and it's already worth $43,000 as I type this. Whilst I never intend on selling it, as it's my dream watch, it's returned a healthy 34 per cent profit.

Risk: low to medium.
Investment timeline: short to medium to long term.

Cars – These are relatively easy to buy, but a purchase can take a few days to a week or so, and do often require you to physically attend a showroom to sign paperwork, even if buying with cash. They also rarely appreciate in value and the best you should often expect is to either lose a small amount, or break even, depending of course on the car you select. A brand new Porsche for $75,000, like I bought for my Dad a few months ago, has already lost me money, but I didn't buy it for investment purposes. I bought it to make him happy and to get some cash out of the bank to de-risk it. A classic Ferrari, on the other hand, bought at $250,000 will likely hold its worth, or thereabouts, and will be a very fun asset to own and drive.

Risk: medium to high.
Investment timeline: medium to long term.

Can you see how most of these investments are medium to long term when it comes to their investment timelines? Investing to de-risk your money and to build wealth is a long-term game.

Also, always keep in mind how liquid the asset is, and make sure that you do not either put all of your eggs in one basket, or put all of your money into one illiquid asset that means you cannot quickly get the cash back if you need it. I suggest always keeping at least six months' of both business and personal expenses in cash in the bank so that you're safe if anything, like it did to Jamie, happens.

Action points

The vehicle you choose will suit the amount of money you have to invest, and the asset or assets you want to pursue. Some people do not like watches or cars and will focus on real estate and index funds. Some people love watches and cars and will buy a Patek Phillippe and a Rolls Royce before they invest in real estate or index funds. I suggest pairing your investments with what you love, and always maintaining a long-term investment horizon.

Chapter 14

CEO Daily Workflow

If you've followed everything I've shared so far in this book, it's highly likely that you are now a CEO. Navigating life as a CEO can be tricky – there will always be something to do and many tasks clamouring for your attention. So now let's cover the "daily CEO workflow" that I provide to my business coaching clients in order to help them prioritise tasks, know what to focus on, and when, and in what specific order. This workflow is the glue that will hold your business together as you scale, helping you to stay focused on what matters most.

1. **CASH FLOW** *[most important thing]*

- Observe net cash flow: total cash in, versus total cash out.

- Monitor the main business bank account, ad spend and total expenses.
- Look at these daily to understand the pulse of each.

• Observe month-end cash and revenue return-on-investment figures via tracking sheet.

  - Keep an eye on whether the revenue and cash figures are trending up or down.
  - In each instance, ask "why" and always keep notes on any funnel alterations.

    ▪ For example, did we hire a new rep, did we hire a new setter, did we launch new ads, did we change a survey question, did we fire an underperformer etc. Never, ever make a change without noting it on the tracking sheet.

- What is the total cash-in-bank? What are the total monthly expenses? How many months of reserves do we hold? Never, ever go below three months of total expenses, including ad spend, of cash in the bank. Ideally, stay above six months, in respect of both business and personal expenses.
- Build a 12-week cash flow statement.

    - Never forget this: the number one reason that businesses go out of business is because they run out of cash. Therefore, understanding your cash flows is the most important part of operating a successful business.
    - Make a note of all of your monthly business expenses in a spreadsheet. Calculate the total monthly burn rate, which means the total amount of expenses expressed in a dollar figure. Lay out the exact date that each expense is due to be paid, in order, from the first day of the month to the last day of the month.
    - Just by doing that, you are in the top one per cent of business owners globally. You now have a clear understanding of your cash flow and your burn rate and you know what amount of money needs to come in, in order to break even and to turn a profit.

- I like to use a calendar in grid format, with a box for each day of the month. I then insert each expense inside the box of the day it's due to come out. I also like to arrange for expenses to be spaced out weekly, where possible, in order to avoid lots of expenses being due too close together. This helps to balance out the inflow of new cash through sales, and the outgoings of expenses, which keeps the business more stable.

2. **THINGS THAT CONTRIBUTE TO CASH FLOW**

- Are the sales reps' calendars full?

    - If they are not, then...

        (**1**) Do an email broadcast to the lead list directly to the booking calendar.
        (**2**) Send an SMS broadcast to those who haven't received one yet.
        (**3**) Ask reps to set calls during their no-show slots.

- Are ads profitable and generating bookings?

    - If not: Focus on creating new ads, or optimising underperforming funnel steps (see Chapter 10) until you reach at least 1.2x cash-collected to cash-spent inside of the current month.

- Are you producing weekly blog videos on YouTube and emailing them to your list?

  - If not: you're leaving serious yield from ad spend on the table. Content like this is a serious high-margin contributor to ad performance – as are emails in general, retargeting ads, SMS broadcasts and re-offers. These things squeeze the juice out of the leads you're paying for.

3. **OPERATIONS**

- Are customer support tickets getting resolved in under 24 hours, with happiness >80 per cent?
- Are accounts being reconciled daily? Receipts attached to line items, notes, etc.
- Are your core systems running properly? Have you fact-checked all of it recently?

  - Core components are:

    - Ads
    - Funnel
    - CRM and emails
    - Calendar and reminders
    - Your training portal where your course is

- Are your sales reps showing up to calls, completing admin tasks, and converting at >20 per cent?

    – Admin tasks are:

- Following up with pipeline
- Filling out a qualitative report daily
- Completing their tracking sheet data
- Archiving call recordings for you to listen to
- Keeping their email inbox clean and organised

4. **Management**

- Daily report on yesterday's:

    – Bookings
    – Calls
    – Units
    – Revenue
    – Cash
    – Emails
    – Content
    – Actions
    – Meetings

- Plan for today: Are calendars full, what are you hearing, any actions needed today?

    – You should always be asking yourself these questions.

- Make sure that you are conducting a team-wide meeting weekly, along with a meeting with the core departments weekly i.e. a management meeting, a coaching and support meeting, etc. Make sure you are conducting one-to-one calls with individual employees at least once per month to stay in the loop.

    - Book these in for greater ease.
    - Observe people: mood, dress, background, tone, inspiration, vibe, drive.

- Reduce costs: where's the money being spent? How can we remove/reduce this?
- Always keep an eye, and look back, on your P&L (profit and loss).

    - Always keep an eye, and look back, on your ad tracking sheet(s).

- Increase income: where's the money coming from? How can we do more of this?
- Do we need additional talent? How are we going to get it?
- Observe your team's workflow, and your own, to optimise it and reduce complexity.
- Identify the top performers and assign efforts to unblock them to flow more throughput.

5. PRODUCT

- Are our customers happy and getting results? If not, this is an emergency.
- How does our product compare to the competition in the market?
- What does the product innovation roadmap look like? What's ahead?
- What's pissing customers off? What's making them fall in love?

    – Observe this, and do less/more of each.

6. STRATEGIC LONGER-TERM INITIATIVES

- What's the vision/mission and how are we progressing?
- Are we staying true to our core values?
- What's our core competence and are we truly the best in the world at this?
- Where's the market headed, what's the consensus reaction, how are we ten steps ahead?
- Do we have a flywheel and is it working?

    – Are clients referring others?
    – Are people buying from us more than once?
    – Are people leaving positive reviews, more than negative reviews?

- How can we make the company more like a self-sustaining ecosystem?

  - Organic content
  - Zero key-man-risk present
  - Team members suggest friends for employment
  - Product keeps getting better, deeper, more impactful

Key words and phrases explained:

- **Key man risk:** Having only one person doing one very important task within your business. For example, if you have only one sales rep and they are responsible for all of your income, if they leave you, your business will instantly need to pause, and so will your income – this is key man risk. Make sure that you always, where possible, have at least two people for each role so that they "hedge" each other, which means providing a back-up.

- **Flywheel:** This means having things that create positive feedback and grow your business for you automatically. For example, word-of-mouth creates a positive flywheel, as does having sales reps that are so happy that they tell all of their friends how good your company is to work for, which leads to other great reps asking for jobs, which saves you from needing to spend your time, money and energy finding and interviewing candidates when you need a new team member, and so on. Another example is

Amazon.com, who because of their low prices and
excellent service, slowly drove all – or most – competitors
out of the market, meaning that their market share rose
and rose, as a positive flywheel, eventually making them
number one. You should look to create positive flywheels
wherever possible.

- **Cash flow**: This means cash coming in and going out
of your business, through sales, advertising spend, staff
costs, and so on. The number one reason that businesses
fail is due to a lack of well-managed cash flow. People
waste money, ignore or overlook costs and do not stay
on top of their unit economics. I implore you to always
watch your cash flow and take it extremely seriously. As

we discussed in Chapter 11, make sure that your LTV is above – ideally, well above – your CPA.

Action points

When you look at that workflow, how much of it are you already doing? If you're not already doing most, if not all, of what I've outlined here, focus on the list, starting at the top. As I've said, cash flow is the most important thing to watch as a business owner. If you're relatively new to this world, I recommend creating your 12-week cash flow statement as soon as possible. Maybe even grab yourself some paper and get started on that now.

Chapter 15

Exit

"We will all sell, one way or another".

Read the above twice over – we will all sell our businesses, one way or another.

Don't worry, I didn't understand that either when I first heard it. What it means, as my mentor Dan Bradbury once said to me, is if you do not sell your business, you are effectively choosing to buy your business for another year or longer. You are choosing to keep running it, when it could otherwise be sold to someone else.

It's an interesting paradox isn't it? If you don't sell your business, you've essentially chosen to buy it and keep running it. Here's the thing, every single business on earth today, big or small,

successful or unsuccessful, profitable or unprofitable *can* be sold. The only question is, at what price. That's the deciding factor.

Think about it, in times of deep recession, many businesses are sold for just £1.

Why? To offload them and close them down, for whatever reason, to someone else who feels that they can take the assets and either grow them, recreate them, or rebuild them. Or perhaps the buyer believes they can achieve something incredible using the remaining bits and pieces of an unsuccessful business.

Let's come back to what I just said though, specifically, "The only question is, at what price?"

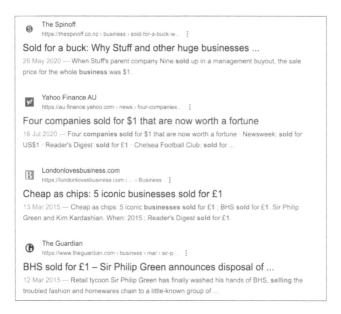

The Spinoff
https://thespinoff.co.nz › business › sold-for-a-buck-w... ⋮

Sold for a buck: Why Stuff and other huge businesses ...

26 May 2020 — When Stuff's parent company Nine **sold** up in a management buyout, the sale price for the whole **business** was $1.

Yahoo Finance AU
https://au.finance.yahoo.com › news › four-companies... ⋮

Four companies sold for $1 that are now worth a fortune

16 Jul 2020 — Four **companies sold** for $1 that are now worth a fortune · Newsweek: **sold** for US$1 · Reader's Digest: **sold** for £1 · Chelsea Football Club: **sold** for ...

Londonlovesbusiness.com
https://londonlovesbusiness.com › ... › Business ⋮

Cheap as chips: 5 iconic businesses sold for £1

13 Mar 2015 — Cheap as chips: 5 iconic **businesses sold** for £1 ; BHS **sold** for £1. Sir Philip Green and Kim Kardashian. When: 2015 ; Reader's Digest **sold** for £1.

The Guardian
https://www.theguardian.com › business › mar › sir-p... ⋮

BHS sold for £1 – Sir Philip Green announces disposal of ...

12 Mar 2015 — Retail tycoon Sir Philip Green has finally washed his hands of BHS, **selling** the troubled fashion and homewares chain to a little-known group of ...

Again, that is the deciding factor. If you build a great business and you structure it for sale by removing yourself from key operations, and having a great track record of sales and client success, then you'll likely be able to sell for a tidy amount. If, on the other hand, you do not build a great business, or it's one that relies heavily on you to operate or is tied directly to your name and face, then you'll still be able to sell it, but for much less than if you'd done the things I just mentioned.

I strongly encourage you to build a saleable business that you can exit one day for a large, life-changing payday, like I did myself. I sold my e-learning company to a US private equity firm for multiple millions of dollars. It was a long, arduous process, but it was all worth it in the end.

I sold my business because I felt I'd outgrown it, as I mentioned earlier in the book. It was no longer fun or exciting to build. I started the business to get rich, build wealth and create a large enough passive income to live on without needing to "work" ever again. I was also excited about it and found the learning and building fun. The minute I had achieved that, five years into the business, a switch flicked off in my head. It was like a tap was turned on one moment, pouring out energy, excitement, drive and focus, and then when I achieved what I'd wanted, that tap was abruptly turned off. I couldn't find a way – no matter what I tried – to turn it back on.

I'd started my business with those goals, and when I hit them, I had no reason to own the business any longer. Thankfully, through sheer luck two years prior, my mentor Dan Bradbury had taught me how to prepare it for sale – by keeping good accounting records, a good track record of profitability, good customer results, happy staff members that stayed for the long-term, and removing myself from operations – which then allowed me to sell the business by working with a mergers and acquisitions (M&A) advisor who found me a buyer.

Seven months later, I walked away with a multi-million dollar exit having sold to a private equity firm.

So, who will you sell to? Yourself, or someone else? Will you sell for $1 or for $1,000,000 plus? It's your decision to make, and whilst it might feel intimidating now at the start of your journey, it will come around quickly. Here's my advice, based on what I've learned in doing all of this myself.

Build your business so it's saleable, and then decide whether to sell or not. Build a great business, with an awesome product, happy customers, great team members, expert accounting and bookkeeping, and then remove yourself from all of the operations you do not love, only working on those you do love. If, at that moment, you want to sell, then do so. You might, however, find that you've built a self-sustaining company that you love to own, and that makes you a great income. If so, do not sell.

Either way, if you can get to this moment, you've achieved what I consider massive success.

At this moment, you might now be thinking, *how is a business valued? How much can I sell my business for?* Valuations are based on many factors such as the market at the time, the economy at the time, the perceived value of your niche or industry at the time, how long you've been in business, how profitable your company is, your direct involvement in the company, whether you sell recurring-income products like a software, or one-time-income products like an online course, and so on. So it's impossible for me to say at what multiple you'll sell your business for.

What I can do, however, is share what I've learned. Recurring-income businesses sell for wildly more than one-time-income

businesses – even if they are not profitable. Yes, even if operating the business actively loses money and they are running on investor capital that's fast going down.

In fact, one of the top things that the private equity firm who bought my business loved was our recurring software. This was a plug-in for a popular trading platform called MetaTrader and when connected, it meant that our trading strategy entry and exit points were plotted on-screen. It was a great tool that our customers loved. We charged $297 per month for it and it was an asset that excited the firm.

Another thing to keep in mind, and something that will affect your exit price, is *who* buys your business. As an example, you might sell your business to a much larger competitor who already has an amazing sales team, an accounting department and so on, and all they want is your amazing product to sell to their existing lead or customer database. Or, you might sell to a private equity firm who know of strategies for growth that you do not, and who will come in, double your business and sell it on for a profit. Their knowledge, capabilities and strategies will inform how much they're able to buy you for.

Equally, you might want to wait for a year or two to sell at a huge price by waiting for the exact right buyer for you, or you might be happy with a much lower price and be able to, therefore, quickly exit in three or four months because "any buyer will do".

Here are the factors I have, through experience, learned are most important to a buyer:

- **Clean, well-organised and simple financial records and bookkeeping.** If a prospective buyer can easily understand the financial performance of your business, and on top of that, it's very easy to verify when in the due-diligence phase of a purchase, you'll sail through an exit in much less time and, in some cases, for much more money, too.
- **Recurring revenue.** This is gold to a buyer. A predictable, sustainable, repeatable source of revenue will find you exiting for as high as a 10x, 20x or even 30x multiple of net profit, if not higher. Buyers dislike businesses that "start from zero each month". These can

certainly still be sold, and my business was of this kind, so I know for a fact that they can be sold. But they will sell for far less money than a company with a wealth of recurring, sustainable revenue, especially if the churn rate is low and customers stick to the subscription.

- **Time in business.** This one is obvious. Would you rather buy a new, unproven business that's been running for one or two years? Or a powerhouse that's grown steadily across five or six years plus, and has proven its place within its respective industry? It is, of course, the latter.

- **Non-involvement of the founder.** To provide an example, three weeks before closing, the private equity firm asked me, "How was last month?" I proceeded to explain that it was one of our best of the year, and they asked me to explain why. I told them that it was down to two things. One being our sales team manager doubling up on performance reviews which raised sales team performance. The other being my having spent 50+ hours building a new webinar that brought us a ton of extremely qualified calls that closed like clockwork. They were not overly pleased with the latter. They did not want to see that business performance rested on me. I had to explain to them that a talented copywriter could have built the webinar, and that I only did it out of passion, because I love writing copy. Thankfully, they let this slide based on that latter fact. My point being buyers do not want a business that rests on its founder's sole involvement. Be sure to remove yourself from operations as much as is possible in order to achieve the best multiple for your exit.

Another thing to mention is how long selling a business takes. On average, it takes between three and nine months, depending on the size of the sale value and who you're selling to. If you're selling to, let's say your business partner, obviously there will be little due diligence to do and you will likely have the exit wrapped up in two or three months. If on the other hand you're selling to a private equity firm or other serious high-level acquirer, expect the due diligence period to be extremely exhaustive and in-depth, therefore, taking many months.

My hope is that by sharing what I've learned here in this short chapter, you will firstly understand that you can sell your business in the future, and secondly you'll understand exactly how to do this as you move forwards and continue building your great business.

Action points

If this has made you start to think about exiting your business, then consider how you can remove yourself from the operations of your company. What tasks can you delegate to one of your team, or are there any hires you need to make in order to lift yourself out of the business as much as possible? The sooner you start thinking about these possibilities, the better, because it allows you to plan properly for them.

If you would like me to mentor you through a sale, like my mentor Dan Bradbury and my M&A advisor Dominic did for me, I would love to help you by having you become a part of my business coaching program, which you can apply for by going to:

www.howtotenmillion.com/join

Chapter 16

You

As a business owner you are a different kind of person, and that means you function differently. But what are the functions of a successful business owner? What I share in this chapter is based on my own experiences of being in that position.

Sacrifice

One of my mentors, Sam Ovens, once said to me, *"You either sacrifice for your goals and dreams, or your goals and dreams become the sacrifice."* I don't need to explain what Sam meant by this, and before we go any further, I'd like to apologise in advance if I cause any offence in this segment of the book, because this is a belief I live by and believe immensely in.

I have sacrificed everything to get to where I am today – fully financially free for life, multi-millionaire, owner of multiple businesses all of which are seven if not eight figures in size, living in an apartment that I own outright in Dubai overlooking the ocean, flying business-class or first-class, wearing a $43,000 solid gold Rolex, with my dream partner, able to travel anywhere, any time, at will.

It was not always like this. To get here I missed weddings, funerals, birthdays and stag parties. I lost many friends along the way. I frustrated family members. I endured a lot of doubt and judgement and, in some cases, hate from others.

There have been incredibly painful and frustrating times over the last six or seven years, since I first started my e-learning company from my parents' spare bedroom with about $8,000 to my name and no outside investment or knowledge whatsoever. All I had was massive ambition and a dream, fumbling around and boot-strapping every element of what I've now built.

But it was all worth it.

You will have to make many sacrifices on your path towards making millions of dollars through your online education company. I was once on a coaching call with Sam, where he genuinely told a member of the mastermind to leave his girlfriend, sell his car, quit his side job and move city to continue growing his business, with complete focus and with no distractions. The guy he told that to, whom I won't name, is now running a multi-eight-figure company four years on and he regularly tells that story of Sam's advice, and how crucial it was to him achieving what he has.

You may need to end your relationship with your girlfriend or boyfriend if it is not conducive to you focusing and building towards achieving your dreams. You might need to quit, or even get, a side job if it's required. You might need to move city, or even country, as I did when I moved from England to Dubai to fuel the growth of my e-learning company and to build a better network of other entrepreneurs. You might need to invest large sums in yourself through joining a mastermind or working with a coach or a mentor in order to get the knowledge you need to scale to the next level.

You must do what is required to achieve your goals and dreams – whatever that is. In not doing so – not taking the leap of faith – your goals and dreams will become the sacrifice you make in order to keep the life you have now, right at this moment, as you read this book.

If you are someone who, as Sam used to say, can "let it all burn", can "throw it all on the fire" and "burn the bridges" in order to achieve your dreams, then I have 100 per cent belief that you will get there. The knowledge on how to build an amazing business is out there – hell, you're reading it, here in this book – but you must trust it and act on it, like the person I just mentioned did when Sam told him what was required to get to the next level.

Invest in knowledge from those who are where you want to be, and do exactly as they say. It's that simple. That truly is the secret to success – find the people who have what you want and soak up their knowledge, observe their actions, do what they do, and you will achieve the same.

Beliefs

Let's strip that last point back – what is the point of investing in knowledge from people who are ahead of you and who have what you desire to have? It is to soak up their beliefs, to understand what they do, to learn how they think and how they operate so that you can emulate them, in order to walk the same – or a similar – path, and thus end up where they've ended up, achieve what they've achieved, and so on.

The first step is deciding what you want. If you are reading this book, I will presume that you want to achieve something similar to what I have. To help you get there, I am sharing everything – literally, every single thing – that you need to know, do, believe and build in order to get there.

All you need to do is listen, learn and then take "massive, messy action" as one of my mentors once called it. Get the knowledge, act on the knowledge. That is your only job, and the results will follow.

Physical health

But it's all for nothing without physical health. Do you sometimes need to sacrifice health to "sprint" and get lots of important work done? Yes, you do. But the last thing you want is to wind up a multi-millionaire with crippling anxiety, overweight, carrying immense stress and unable to enjoy everything you've built.

I am a big believer in having priorities, listed in order. My number one priority is my career and building great businesses, along with creating wealth, and helping others achieve the same for themselves, hence why I've invested over 250+ hours writing this book to help you. This comes, for me, above relationships or even health, but I am not foolish enough to let those two aspects of a healthy, fulfilling life lay to waste.

They may not be my number one priority, but they are second and third in line and I pay them the respect and attention that they deserve. I have a personal trainer who I see every morning five days per week, a treadmill desk so I can walk and work, and a great girlfriend who I love.

But I have made it very clear to both, they come second to my work – priorities and sacrifice.

Mental health

This is all we have and I place it way above physical health. If you know me personally, you'll nod your head as you read this in agreement, but I am huge on focus. Cut out everything that you do not want or need physically, forget about everything that is not important mentally, and focus only and whole-heartedly on the things that you do want and need. I call it "keeping my brain clean".

I do this very intentionally. A couple of the tools I use are firstly journalling, and secondly meditation.

Dropping knowledge: journal to supercharge your life

Journalling is the single most powerful tool you can use to empty your mind, calm your emotions and create mental clarity, peace and focus. If you do not journal, begin immediately. Buy a journal and, every few days, pause to write out the date and what's on your mind, what you are working on, what's worrying you and why, whether you are heading towards your main goals and, if not, then why not and how will you get back on track, and what your main goals are. Always be aware of your next three goals, listed in order of importance, along with the precise steps you're taking to achieve them – your current financial situation, all cash on-hand, where your investments are positioned, and so on.

All of the most important info is written in your journal. Make sure that your journal is either hidden where no-one can find it, or if you leave it on your desk, make anyone who may enter your office aware that they should never, ever read it. This is because if you have the slightest feeling that your journal entries will be read by others, you will not be completely honest with yourself in your writing, due to fear of judgement.

I want to also admit something about myself here. If I'm ever asked to do anything that's not a priority, something that is outside of my key areas of focus, I am very lazy in responding, I will likely cancel last minute, and I will not prepare ahead of time. Why? Because my brain is laser-focused on my priorities, 90 per cent of my energy and thought is on my goals and dreams. Leaving only 10 per cent spare for "other" activities like watching television, cleaning and cooking, nipping to the shop to buy a sandwich, and so on.

That's how, I believe, I've gotten to where I am today – full focus at all times.

I do not have children, a wife, or 25 friends. I do not go out on weekends, I very rarely go on holiday, or even travel further than a one-mile radius from where I live. In fact I barely leave my apartment, depending on what I'm working on and when. I am 100 per cent consumed by making my dreams a reality, building what I love to build – this book, for example – whilst keeping my mind as clean as possible in the process, to further fuel that focus.

Do I make time for fun? Absolutely, you must. Every once in a while I go downstairs and jet ski, relax and read on the beach, go for a long walk, or go out for coffee or dinner with friends. It's important to be a human, but to reach incredible levels of success, you have to be different from most people – you have to prioritise, sacrifice and focus.

If you do what normal people do, you get what normal people get, which is nothing. If you do what extraordinary people do, you get what extraordinary people get, which is anything you desire, because you will work tirelessly until it's yours.

Finite time

But, stay aware of time. For God's sake, stay aware of time.

Time is all we have. Bill Gates and Warren Buffett have 24 hours in a day, just like I do, just like you do. As I type this, it's Saturday at 3:45pm. My only focus for today is another five to seven hours of writing this book, I have no other plans whatsoever. At the moment, all of my time, energy and focus is being poured into making this book as incredible as I can make it for you, so that I ensure I'm able to get you the absolute best results possible.

How do you use your time currently? What do you *use* it on, and what do you *waste* it on? Be honest, be brutally honest. This would make a good section within your journal. In fact, write the question out and spend 30 minutes of your time – this is a great use of your time – getting clear on where your time goes, specifically. I suggest bucketing it into two, well, buckets, one being "time wasted on unimportant tasks" and two being "time invested in important tasks".

I'd also like to share an exercise that Sam Ovens shared with me: 100 units of time.

In this exercise you again take your journal, and for every single hour of the day that you are awake, you set an alarm to go off every 30 minutes for the entire day. Every time it goes off, you must write down exactly what you've been doing. Writing, reading, meditating, working, exercising, cleaning, using social media, creating content, shopping, crying because you've just realised how much work you've got lying ahead of you in order to become a billionaire – OK, the last one might just be me, but you get the point.

Then, after one full week of doing this, you'll create two buckets: time wasted and time invested. The good and the bad. What did you waste time on, that is not moving you closer towards your goals and dreams? What did you invest time in, that is moving you closer towards your goals and dreams?

Stop doing the bad, and do more of the good. Where possible, outsource things that do not move the needle as much as other things. Hire someone to do your food shopping, create content for your social media, clean your home, or manage your inbox, and so on.

Free up your time so that you can invest more of it in the all-important tasks that move the needle in the most impactful way for you and your goals and dreams. Time is all we have, and we won't be given more of it. Do not waste it. The time is now.

Finite focus

Similar to time, we only have so much focus to use each day.

Let me ask you a question, have you ever had an internet browser running with a ridiculous amount of tabs open? I'm talking three, five, ten tabs open? What happens in that scenario? Your computer almost grinds to a halt because it can't handle the load. It runs out of energy.

Humans are no different. We can only focus on so many things at one time.

You know that awake and focused feeling you have when you sit down to start a day of exciting work? That's the beginning of your focused energy for the day. On the other side of the coin, you know that groggy and tired feeling you have when it's the end of a gruelling day of hard work? That's the end of your focused energy for the day.

Just like we have only 24 hours of time, we only have let's say 'x' units of focus within us, and these units slowly wear down and erode with each passing hour of hard work. They drain out of you like water from a dam as time passes, so it's critical to make sure that you are only working on what will truly move the needle. Ideally, working on the most important tasks first, and leaving the less important ones for later, if not outsourcing them entirely.

Another way to dramatically increase focus is to only do one thing, two maximum, per day. For example my singular focus for today is writing this book, and otherwise, I'll only relax – maybe have a swim later on, do some reading, or go for a cigar and a whiskey – but nothing strenuous that requires absolute uninterrupted focus. The worst way to destroy focus is with a huge to-do list featuring a mix of tasks that vary in importance.

What one single thing do you need to do next, after putting this book down, to move you closer towards your goals and dreams? If you need to make an opt-in page, write a sales video, or create a sales script, just go and do it.

Shut the door, lock the windows, turn your phone off, and do it.

Alchemy of Self

What I'm about to share here has absolutely changed my life. I know that might sound overly dramatic, but it really has. Just wait until you have your own "Alchemy of Self" document – it is truly a game-changer. My "Alchemy of Self" document is the most important document I've ever created and I live by it.

The full document is on my desktop at all times, the vision-board aspect of the document is printed out, laminated and is on the wall around my apartment – on the mirror, on the fridge, and so on. The document itself lays out my biggest, hairiest, most audacious goals, in order of achieving them, both past and present, so I can track my journey, along with the written step-by-step plan to achieve them. Each goal is accompanied by a black square, which you replace with an image, only when you've attained the goal.

The first goal on there is "professional musician". That's where my story starts. From there, the next is "started trading" and then "began my e-learning company", followed by "bought my first apartment" and "won the Two Comma Club Award", then "became a millionaire" and so on.

The goals you'll put on here are a mix of personal and professional, and you'll lay them out in order of achieving them. They form the past and present parts – steps, almost – of your journey as a whole. Often, one goal will lead into, or lay the foundation for, others as you progress. I encourage you to plan at least five goals ahead, and as you begin achieving them you'll build up more and more momentum, which will help you to dream bigger and bigger as you prove to yourself that you can achieve anything you put your mind, time and focus into.

Aside from goals, your "Alchemy of Self" document will include three other things. The first is your affirmations that are unique to you. Affirmations are a script that describes what you want your future to look like, but are written as if you've already achieved everything. They are scientifically proven to speak to your subconscious mind and what your subconscious mind believes, leads to what your conscious mind begins taking steps to physically achieve.

The second thing it includes is your "ideal character" worksheet which will describe, in detail, who you need to be and become to make achieving your dreams effortless. This will include the habits you have, the clothes you wear, the location you live in, your health status, how you behave and treat others – everything will be laid out to allow you to understand precisely who you need to become to achieve everything you've ever wanted.

The third thing it includes is a vision board. Some people think that creating a vision board is cheesy or doesn't work. If that is you, that's OK. If you don't believe in something, you are making sure that you will prevent yourself from achieving it, or progressing towards it, and I am not here to convince you to change. All I can do is share what's worked for me and almost every wealthy person I know, and that is having a document like this along with a vision board. I urge you to trust me and to create one for yourself, inside your own "Alchemy of Self" document, by taking images and putting them together to form a collage that visually represents your dream life and everything you want to achieve.

This document, when built out completely, will be your "dream life blueprint". When you've created it, it will spur an energy in you that you've never experienced before and it will begin to pull you towards your goals and dreams, due to the absolute clarity you've created. That's what a document like this does – it creates complete clarity, and it allows you to understand

not only where you're going and what you're building, but when, how, in what order, and so on.

It is a very powerful document.

Download my "Alchemy of Self" template and create your own at:

www.howtotenmillion.com/resources

Action points

If you only take one thing from this chapter, make it the "Alchemy of Self" document. The sooner you begin mapping out how you want your dream life to look, the sooner you will find you are on the road to achieving it. There is very powerful psychology that supports this approach and, as I've said, it has not only worked for me, but a great many other highly successful people. I urge you to try it for yourself.

Conclusion

If you've read this book in full, that in itself is a massive achievement. Most people never invest in their knowledge or growth, let alone take action after doing so. You are different. You're like me. You'll stop at nothing to make your goals and dreams a reality. Full focus at all times, no matter what.

Throughout this book, I have genuinely shared everything I've learned and used to make over $20,000,000 in total sales revenue over the last seven years. I have not "hidden" anything, or "kept anything secret" so you need to buy anything from me. I have held nothing back. You now know everything that I know and have learned. I've spent well over $250,000 on coaches, courses, mentors and masterminds. You've been handed all of it in this book. It's all in here.

If you act on everything I've given you and taught you, if you build what needs to be built, if you work hard and with focus and consistency, you're going to have a lot of fun, make a lot of money, and add massive value for the clients and customers you serve.

I'm excited for you, and here's to your success.

If you would like to learn more about working with me as a business coach, you'll find everything you need to know here:

www.howtotenmillion.com/join

You'll have noticed that I've shared links to resources throughout the book, too. To save you time and effort searching for them, everything you need is on these two web pages:

www.howtotenmillion.com/resources

www.howtotenmillion.com/join

About the Author

William Brown is a lifelong entrepreneur.

He started his first business at the age of 15, and with every venture that followed – from international record producer and DJ, to trading financial markets – he became more and more successful and ambitious. At 27, he founded his e-learning company, scaling it to $16.4 million in total sales revenue within five years. He successfully sold this company to a private equity firm in 2023.

While building his incredibly successful business, William invested his money into real estate, building a holding company worth multiple seven figures. After the sale of his e-learning company, William found a new purpose – helping other entrepreneurs in the e-learning space achieve the same levels of success he has.

He currently lives between his homes in England and Dubai, and runs his newly-founded consulting company www. buildgrowandexit.com, which helps new and existing e-learning business owners to build their company, grow their company or exit their company, using what he learned from doing all three over the last decade.

Made in United States
Troutdale, OR
11/05/2024

24470224R00189